# SOYMILK DESSERTS

**Distributed by JAPAN PUBLICATIONS TRADING CO., LTD**

**Distributors:**

**UNITED STATES:** Kodansha America, Inc., through Oxford University Press, 198 Madison Avenue, New York, NY 10016

**CANADA:** Fitzhenry & Whiteside Ltd., 195 Allstate Parkway, Markham, Ontario L3R 4T8

**UNITED KINGDOM AND EUROPE:** Premier Book Marketing Ltd., Clarendon House, 52, Cornmarket Street, Oxford, OX1 3HJ England

**AUSTRALIA AND NEW ZEALAND:** Bookwise International, 174 Cormack Road, Wingfield, SA 5013 Australia

**ASIA & JAPAN:** Japan Publications Trading Co., Ltd., 1-2-1, Sarugaku-cho, Chiyoda-ku, Tokyo 101-0064 Japan

First printing: February 2004    Original Copyright ©2004 by Yasuyo Shida
World rights reserved. Published by JOIE, INC. 1-8-3, Hirakawa-cho, Chiyoda-ku, Tokyo 102-0093 Japan    Printed in Japan
ISBN 4-88996-168-2

**NOTES**

This book uses the following measurements for volume:

**1 level teaspoon (tsp) : 5 ml**
**1 level tablespoon (Tbsp) : 15 ml**
**1 cup : 240 ml**

The cooking time given in this book is based on a 600W microwave oven, used at high power.

The baking time and temperature given in this book indicate only a rough standard. You might need to adjust them depending on your oven especially when it comes to dessert baking.

The egg used in this book is a medium to small size egg.

Preparation time shown in this book excludes preheating the oven, cooling or freezing heated ingredients, thawing, baking or steaming. Read the recipes thoroughly and match the recipe to the free time you have.

## ABOUT THE AUTHOR

**Yasuyo Shida**, who explored her interest in confectionary art by studying at both L'Ecole Lenotre in Paris, France and at Richmond Bakery School in Luzern, Switzerland, has been actively appearing on TV and magazines as a notable confection studier as well as teaching at her home, salon style. Her easily made yet sophisticated confections are highly praised among gourmets of all generations in Japan.

# Contents

# BAKED DESSERTS

# STEAMED/ FRIED DESSERTS

# FRUIT DESSERTS

# CHILLED DESSERTS

# DRINKS & SHAKES

# BAKED DESSERTS

This chapter introduces a selection of flavorful puddings, cakes, pastries and cookies, all featuring soymilk, *tofu*, and other soyfoods.

# Moist Chocolate Cake

**A rich, moist chocolate cake baked with sour cream topping. Enjoy the luxurious contrast of both flavor and color.**

## Ingredients

3¹/₂ oz (100g)  baking chocolate
3¹/₂ oz (100g)  unsalted butter
4 Tbsp  powdered sugar
2 eggs, separated
2 oz (60g)  ground almonds
40 ml  soymilk
1³/₄ oz (50g)  all purpose flour
1 Tbsp  cocoa powder
1⁵/₆ oz (55g) granulated sugar
Cream topping
  4 oz (120g)  sour cream
  2 Tbsp  soymilk
  3 Tbsp  powdered sugar
  2 Tbsp  cornstarch
**(for 7" baking pan)**

Difficulty Level ★★★
Prep time: 20 minutes

### Do-Ahead Tips
◆Preheat oven to 325℉(160℃).
◆Let butter and eggs stand at room temperature.
◆Sift powdered sugar.
◆Sift together flour and cocoa.

## Directions

① Shred chocolate, and heat in a double boiler, stirring with a wooden spatula until melted.

② In a separate bowl, cream butter with a whisk. Add sifted powdered sugar, and whisk until the mixture turns light in color.

③ Add egg yolks, one at a time, stirring well after each addition. Stir in crumbled ground almonds and soymilk.

④ Add melted chocolate and stir well.

⑤ In a clean bowl, place egg whites and a pinch of sugar. Whisk until runny. Add remaining sugar and whisk until stiff.

⑥ Fold in ¹/₃ of sifted flour and cocoa mixture using a rubber spatula. Add another ¹/₃ portion when some of the flour still remains. Mix lightly and repeat with the remaining portion. This time, mix until no flour is visible.

⑦ Using your finger, dab the mixture at several points of the parchment to secure it to the baking pan. Pour the mixture into baking pan, and bake 30 to 35 minutes at 325℉ (160℃).

⑧ Make cream topping. Sift together powdered sugar and cornstarch. Blend sour cream with soymilk. Add sifted sugar mixture gradually, and mix well until smooth.

⑨ Spread cream over the top of cooled chocolate cake, and bake at 400℉(200℃) for 3 to 5 minutes. Refrigerate before serving.

# Tofu Cheesecake

**Not too rich cheesecake made with *tofu* and apricots.**

Difficulty Level ★★★

Prep time: 25 minutes

## Ingredients

2¹/₃ Tbsp  unsalted butter, melted
2¹/₈ oz (70 g)  graham crackers
Melted unsalted butter for greasing
7 canned apricots
Filling:
  7 oz (200 g) cream cheese
  7 tsp unsalted butter
  3¹/₂ oz (100 g)  granulated sugar
  1 egg, beaten
  ¹/₂ cake soft *tofu*
  2 Tbsp  lemon juice
  2 Tbsp  all purpose flour
  2 Tbsp  cornstarch

**(for 6" spring-form baking pan)**

## Do-Ahead Tips

◆Slice canned apricots; drain. Drain *tofu*.
◆Soften cream cheese and butter at room temperature.
◆Sift flour and cornstarch together.
◆Preheat oven to 320℉ (160℃).

## Directions

① In a large bowl, blend melted butter and crushed graham crackers. Butter the baking pan, and line the bottom with round-cut parchment.

② Press crust mixture into the pan, using the back of a spoon. Refrigerate about 30 minutes.

③ Make filling. In a bowl, mix softened cream cheese and butter. Whisk until smooth, and then stir in granulated sugar, divided into two portions.

④ When the mixture turns light in color, add beaten eggs gradually, one-fourth at a time. Continue beating.

⑤ Add drained *tofu* and lemon juice. Then beat in sifted powder sugar.

⑥ Arrange apricot slices over the crust. Pour in filling, and bake at 320℉ (160℃) for 20 minutes. Turn up the heat to 350℉(180℃) and bake for 15 - 20 minutes until golden. Remove from the oven and let cool in the pan. When almost cooled, remove from the pan and chill at least 4 hours.

# Earl Grey Roulade

**Aromatic tealeaves enhance the richly flavored soymilk custard.**
**Earl Grey is selected for a distinctive flavor.**

Difficulty Level ★★

Prep time: 20 minutes

## Ingredients

3 egg whites

5 egg yolks

3 oz (85 g)  granulated sugar

3 Tbsp  unsalted butter, melted

5 Tbsp  all purpose flour

1 fine black tea bag

1 cup  soymilk custard (see page 19)

**(for 12" square baking tray)**

## Do-Ahead Tips

◆ Sift flour and mix with tea leaves.

◆ Let eggs stand at room temperature.

◆ Preheat oven to 375°F(190℃).

◆ Make soymilk custard.

## Directions

① Make meringue. Whisk egg whites until foamy and thickened. Add half of the sugar, and whisk until a stiff peak is formed when lifted.

② Beat egg yolks with the remaining sugar in a bowl over hot water. Beat until light in color and thick in texture.

③ Beat in melted butter. Whisk well, incorporating air.

④ Fold in half of the meringue by turning a rubber spatula only about 5 times. Fold in half of the flour mixture gently, stirring only about 7 times by writing a figure 8. When some flour is still visible, fold in remaining meringue in the same manner. Finally fold in remaining flour mixture, until the flour is invisible.

⑤ Line baking tray with a parchment. Pour in sponge dough. Using a spatula, smooth out the surface. Bake at 375°F(190℃) for 10 minutes. Remove from the oven, and cover with a piece of parchment. Turn upside down and put on a cake cooler. Gently remove the upper parchment. Let stand to cool.

⑥ Peel off browned surface of the sponge. Make 4-5 scores from an edge of the sponge, by pressing a spatula as shown. This makes the sponge easy to be rolled.

⑦ Spread soymilk custard, leaving out 1" at the near end, and 1/2" at far end. Lift the near edge, and fold it tightly to start the roll. Roll up, and place rolled edge down.

# Brownies with Tofu Crumble

Enjoy the contrast of rich, walnut brownie and delicate topping, made from *okara*, a by-product of *tofu*.

**Difficulty Level ★★**

**Prep time: 30 minutes**

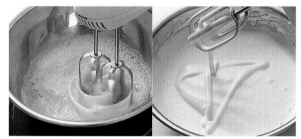

## Ingredients

5$\frac{1}{2}$ oz (150 g) sweet
  baking chocolate
5$\frac{1}{2}$ oz (150 g) unsalted
  butter
3 eggs
$\frac{1}{4}$ cup granulated sugar
$\frac{4}{5}$ cup all purpose flour
1 tsp baking powder
2$\frac{3}{4}$ oz (80g) walnuts,
  chopped
1 Tbsp molasses

*Tofu* Crumble
3 Tbsp unsalted butter
3 Tbsp granulated sugar
1 oz (30 g) *okara* *
7 tsp all purpose flour
1 Tbsp ground almonds

*a by-product of *tofu*

**(for 8" square pan)**

## Do-Ahead Tips

◆Let eggs stand at room temperature.
◆Sift together flour and baking powder together.
◆Roast walnuts, and cut up when cooled.
◆Line baking pan with parchment cut to the bottom size.
◆Preheat oven to 350°F(180°C).

## Directions

① Chop chocolate and butter. Melt them in a bowl over hot water, stirring constantly until smooth.

② In a separate bowl beat eggs, adding granulated sugar. Whisk until the mixture is pale and thick, and holds a trail in a clear ribbon, for about 5 seconds.

③ Divide flour mixture into 2 or 3, and add one portion at a time. Fold in lightly with a rubber spatula after each addition.

④ Fold in chocolate mixture.

⑤ Then fold in walnuts and molasses.

⑥ Make crumble. In a bowl, sieve together flour and ground almonds. Add sugar and *okara*, and mix well. Add cold butter and rub between your palms to resemble coarse breadcrumbs.

⑦ Pour dough into the baking pan, and flatten the surface. Sprinkle with *tofu* crumbles. Bake at 350°F(180°C) for about 30 minutes. Let cool and slice into squares.

# Cheese Soufflé

**A deliciously delicate, fluffy dessert.**
**Great when chilled!**

Difficulty Level ★★

Prep time: 30 minutes

## Ingredients

Cheese mixture
  3¼ oz (90 g)  cream cheese
  1½ Tbsp  unsalted butter,
  1 oz (30 g)  granulated sugar
  1  egg yolk
  3 Tbsp  all purpose flour, sifted
  70 ml  soymilk
Meringue
  1½  egg whites
  2 Tbsp  superfine sugar
Rum raisins
  1½ oz (40 g )  raisins
  1 Tbsp  rum
Powdered sugar, for dusting

### (for 8  2" ring pans)

## Do-Ahead Tips

◆Sprinkle raisins with rum, and let stand at least 30 minutes.
◆Let butter, cream cheese and eggs stand at room temperature.
◆Preheat oven to 300°F (150°C) - 320°F (160°C).

## Directions

① Layer non-stick parchment over an oversized foil. Butter the ring pans. Line the sides of each pan with parchment and place on the layers. Fold up foil to prevent leakage.

② Place 6-7 rum raisins on each bottom.

③ In a bowl, whisk cream and butter. Add sugar and continue beating.

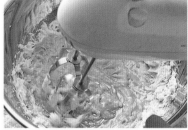

④ Add egg yolk, then flour. Whisk until well blended. Stir in soymilk gradually, beating after each addition.
Make meringue. In a separate bowl, whisk egg white until almost stiff but not completely. Add sugar and whisk until very stiff.

⑤ Add ⅓ portion of the meringue to the cheese mixture, and beat well. Add this to the bowl of remaining meringue, and fold in lightly using a rubber spatula.

⑥ Pour into each pan to ⁷⁄₁₀ full. Place on baking tray, and pour hot water up to the middle of the pans. Cook and steam in the preheated oven for 20 minutes. When almost cooled, remove from pans and dust with powdered sugar.

# Tofu Custard

All-time favorite egg custard using both *tofu* and soymilk.
Deliciously delicate, creamy dessert.

Difficulty Level ★

Prep time: 15 minutes

16

## Ingredients

2³/₄ oz (80 g)  soft *tofu*

250 ml  soymilk

60 ml  heavy/whipping
cream

¹/₃ stick vanilla bean

2  eggs, beaten with
1 egg yolk

3 oz (85 g)  granulated
sugar

**(for 6  2¹/₂" custard
cups)**

## Do-Ahead Tips

◆Grease custard cups
with extra butter.

◆Make caramel syrup
(below) and pour into
individual cups; keep
refrigerated to settle,
for about 10 minutes.

◆Preheat oven to
320℉ (160℃).

## Directions

① Wrap *tofu* in kitchen
towel, and microwave
for 1¹/₂ minutes. Drain
and pass through a
strainer. Set aside.

② In a saucepan heat
soymilk, cream and
broken vanilla bean.
Remove from heat just
below boiling point.

③ In a bowl beat egg
mixture and sugar
until pale. Add sieved
*tofu*, and beat again
until pale.

④ Stir in soymilk
mixture. Pass through
a strainer to make a
smooth texture.
Pour into chilled
custard cups coated
with hardened caramel
syrup.

⑤Line a shallow pan with
wetted paper towel, and
arrange custard cups on it.
Place the pan on baking
tray, and fill with hot
water about ⁷/₁₀ full. Bake
at 320℉ (160℃) for 20-25
minutes until set. Place
the cups in simmering hot
water to unmold.

### Caramel Syrup

2³/₄ oz (80 g)  granulated sugar

20 ml  water

20 ml  boiling water

In a saucepan, heat sugar and
the cold water to boil. Cook and
stir until lightly browned, and
releasing a sweet aroma.
Remove from heat immediately.

Pour in boiling water carefully,
since this may splash the hot
syrup. Wear a cotton glove or
mitten to prevent you from burn.

# Chocolate Pudding

**Rich and smooth pudding easily made in serving cups.
Great when chilled.**

Difficulty Level ★

Prep time: 15 minutes

## Ingredients

1³/₄ oz (50 g)  plain
   chocolate, coarsely
   chopped
4  egg yolks, beaten
250 ml  soymilk
200 ml  heavy/whipping
   cream
1¹/₂ oz (40 g)  granulated
   sugar
50 ml  whipping cream for
   topping

## (serves 6)

## Do-Ahead Tips

◆Make caramel syrup
   (page 17) and pour
   into each cup; chill
   until use.
◆Preheat oven to
   300℉ (150℃).

## Directions

① In a saucepan heat
soymilk and cream just
until it almost reaches
the boiling point.
Remove from heat.

② In a bowl, place
chopped chocolate and
sugar. Stir in hot
soymilk mixture to
melt the chocolate
completely.

③ Pour the mixture
into beaten egg yolks,
and blend well. Pass
through a strainer.

④ Pour the mixture
into the prepared and
chilled cups. Arrange in
a baking tray, and pour
hot water to reach a
quarter height of the
cups. Bake at 300℉
(150℃) for 30-35
minutes until set.
When cooled, lightly
whip cream and pour
into each cup; chill at
least 40 minutes before
serving.

# Millefeuille

**Cream slices with tangy fruits made easy with frozen puff pastry.**

Difficulty Level ★

Prep time: 40 minutes

## Ingredients

1 sheet (8" square) frozen
  puff pastry, thawed
2-3 Tbsp  powdered sugar
Kiwi fruit, sliced
Grapefruit, segmented
Pistachios, chopped
Soymilk custard (See
  below)

## (yields 4)

## Do-Ahead Tips

◆Make soymilk
  custard.
◆Preheat oven to
  375℉(190℃) -
  400℉(200℃).

## Directions

① Over a non-stick
parchment, lay thawed
puff pastry, and cover
with plastic wrap. Roll
out to $^1/_{10}$" thickness.
Remove wrap and place
in baking pan. Prick all
over, and sprinkle with
powdered sugar. Bake
at 375℉(190℃) to
400℉(200℃) for 15-17
minutes, until puffed
and golden.
Cut into the same size
squares.
② Layer puff pastry,
fruits, then soymilk
custard. Top with
another piece of puff
pastry. Sprinkle with
powdered sugar and
chopped pistachios.

### Soymilk Custard

3 egg yolks
5 Tbsp granulated sugar
3 Tbsp all purpose flour
1 cup soymilk
$^1/_2$ stick vanilla bean
1 Tbsp unsalted butter

① In a bowl, whisk egg
yolks and sugar.

② Add sifted flour and
mix well. In a
saucepan, heat
soymilk, and turn off
heat just before boiling.

③ Add soymilk gradually to the bowl. When all
the soymilk is added, put back to the saucepan,
and heat until thickened. Remove from heat
and stir in butter.

④ Transfer to a
shallow baking pan,
cover tightly with plastic
wrap, and let cool.

# Red Bean Cake

**Moist and light sponge studded with sweet bean jam.**

Difficulty Level ★★

Prep time: 20 minutes

## Ingredients (for 1 loaf)

2 eggs, separated

2 oz (55 g)  granulated sugar

$^5/_6$ oz (25 g)  powdered sugar

3 $^1/_6$ oz (95 g)  all purpose flour

1 tsp  baking powder

$^1/_2$ tsp  salt

30 ml  soymilk, blended with
  30 ml  vegetable oil

4$^2/_3$ oz (140 g)  *yude-adzuki*, bean
  jam (canned)

$^1/_4$ oz (10 g)  *amanatto*, sugar-glazed
  *adzuki* beans, optional

## Do-Ahead Tips

◆Let eggs stand at room
  temperature.

◆Sift together flour and baking
  powder.

◆Preheat oven to 340℉ (170℃).

◆Make a mold with a milk carton.

### Instant loaf tin

Wash and dry a milk carton.
Cut away one long side.
Staple ends to secure.

## Directions

① In a bowl, beat egg yolks with
half amount of the granulated
sugar until thickened. Stir in
half amount of the powdered
sugar. Beat well, and add the
remaining powdered sugar.

② When dropping consistency is achieved, fold in bean jam. Combine
soymilk and oil, and stir in the batter.
Make meringue. In a clean bowl, beat egg whites until almost stiff.
Add remaining granulated sugar and whisk until very stiff.

③ Add half of the meringue to the egg mixture and mix lightly. Fold
in half of the flour mixture. When flour is still visible, fold in half of
the sugar-glazed beans. Fold in the remaining meringue, flour
mixture, then remaining beans. Blend well at this final stage.

④ Pour into a milk carton
"mold", and bake at 340℉
(170℃) for 25-30 minutes.

# Scones

**Scones with less sugar make a good brunch as well as a tea companion.**

Difficulty Level ★★

Prep time: 25 minutes

## Ingredients

9 oz (260 g)  all-purpose flour

1 Tbsp  baking powder

1 1/2 Tbsp  granulated sugar

1 3/4 oz (50 g)  unsalted butter

1  egg, beaten

60 ml  soymilk

**(yields 7-8)**

## Do-Ahead Tips

◆Sift together flour and baking powder.

◆Cut butter into cubes, and keep refrigerated.

◆Preheat oven to 340℉ (170℃) - 350℉(180℃).

## Directions

①In a bowl, blend sifted flour mixture and sugar.

② Add chilled butter, and break the butter into the flour using a dough cutter or scraper.

③ Rub between your palms to blend well, until the mixture resembles fine breadcrumbs.

④ Add beaten egg and soymilk and blend well. Press it together without kneading, and wrap in plastic wrap. Refrigerate it at least 30 minutes.

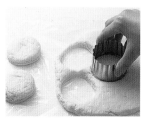

⑤ Roll out to 5/8"-3/4" thickness. Using a 2 1/2" cutter, cut out 8 circles. Brush tops with soymilk (extra) and bake at 340℉ (170℃) - 350℉(180℃) for 20 minutes.

# Tofu and Chocolate Chip Cookies — BAKED DESSERTS

**Fiber-rich, yet crisp shortbread cookies filled with choc, citrus and *okara*.**

**Difficulty Level ★★★**

**Prep time: 30 minutes**

## Ingredients

5$^1$/$_2$ oz (150 g) unsalted butter

2$^1$/$_2$ oz (70 g) granulated sugar

A pinch of salt

1 egg, beaten with 1 egg yolk

1 Tbsp soymilk

3 oz (80 g) *okara**

4 $^3$/$_4$ oz (130 g) all purpose flour

1 tsp baking powder

1 oz (30 g) chopped walnuts

1 oz (30 g) chopped orange peel

1$^1$/$_2$ oz (40 g) chocolate chips

*a by-product of *tofu*

**(yields 20)**

## Do-Ahead Tips

◆ Let butter stand at room temperature.

◆ Sift together flour and baking powder.

◆ Chop up fruits and nuts.

◆ Preheat oven to 340°F (170℃) - 350°F(180℃).

## Directions

① In a bowl, cream the butter with a whisk. Stir in sugar and salt. Beat until light in color.

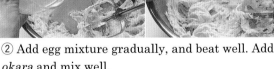

② Add egg mixture gradually, and beat well. Add *okara* and mix well.

③ Stir in flour mixture, and nuts.

④ Press together and chill at least 30 minutes.

⑤ Divide dough into halves. Press each to $^1$/$_{10}$" thickness using your hands. Bake at 340°F (170℃) - 350°F (180℃) for 20-25 minutes, until the surface turns golden. Break into pieces to serve.

# Peanut and Sesame Biscotti

**Crispy cookies studded with peanuts and black sesame seeds for added aroma. There's no need to use any baking mold.**

Difficulty Level ★★

Prep time: 20 minutes

## Ingredients

1 egg, beaten

2$\frac{1}{2}$ oz  granulated sugar

2$\frac{1}{2}$ oz  ground almonds

40 ml  vegetable oil

3 Tbsp  soymilk

Few drops  vanilla oil

5$\frac{1}{2}$ oz (150 g)  all purpose flour,
   sifted with:
   $\frac{1}{2}$ tsp baking powder
   $\frac{1}{8}$ tsp baking soda
   $\frac{1}{8}$ tsp salt

2$\frac{1}{4}$ oz (60 g)   peanuts, chopped

2 Tbsp toasted black sesame seeds

$\frac{1}{2}$  egg white

### (yields 20 slices)

## Do-Ahead Tips

◆ Preheat oven to 340℉(170℃) -
   350℉(180℃).

## Directions

① In a bowl, blend egg and granulated sugar. Stir in ground almonds.

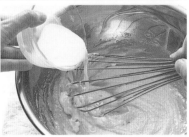

② Swirl in vegetable oil gradually, and beat well until creamy. Stir in soymilk, then vanilla oil.

③ Add sifted dry ingredients, chopped peanuts and toasted sesame seeds. Blend well.

④ Press together and divide into halves. Form each into a log, and place two apart on prepared parchment. Brush on beaten egg white, and bake at 340℉(170℃) - 350℉(180℃) for 30-35 minutes.

⑤ Let cool for 10 minutes. Cut into $\frac{5}{8}$" slices, and put them back into the oven. Bake at the same temperature for 7 minutes. Turn over and bake another 7 minutes.

# Tofu and Pine Nut Drops

**Quick and easy bite-size cookies with dietary fiber and nutritious pine nuts.**

Difficulty Level ★

Prep time: 20 minutes

## Ingredients

4 oz (120 g)  unsalted butter

3½ oz (100g)  granulated sugar

1  egg, beaten

Vanilla extract

1¼ oz (50 g)  *okara**

3¼ oz (90 g)  all purpose flour

1¼ oz (40 g)  pine nuts

*a by-product of *tofu*

**(yields 20)**

## Do-Ahead Tips

◆ Soften butter at room temperature.

◆ Sift flour.

◆ Preheat oven to 340°F(170°C) - 350°F (180°C).

## Directions

① In a bowl, cream the butter until soft.

② Add half amount of sugar, and blend. Stir in remaining sugar.

③ Stir in beaten eggs gradually, at 4-5 times, beating after each addition. Add vanilla extract.

④ Stir in *okara*, then add sifted flour at a time. Fold in pine nuts.

⑤ On prepared baking tray, place spoonful of dough, and bake at 340°F(170°C) - 350°F(180°C) for 12-15 minutes.

# Tofu Cookies

Reminiscent of the *soba-boro*, a traditional buckwheat snack of Kyoto, these flower-shaped cookies blend the richness of butter with a crunch of *okara*.

Difficulty Level ★★★

Prep time: 30 minutes

## Ingredients

1³/₄ oz (50 g)  unsalted butter

3 oz (85g)  granulated sugar

A pinch of salt

1 egg, beaten

4 oz (120 g)  all purpose flour

¹/₂ tsp  baking powder

¹/₂ tsp  baking soda

2³/₄ oz (80 g)  *okara**

Vanilla extract

*a by-product of *tofu*

## (yields 20-22)

## Do-Ahead Tips

◆Let butter and eggs stand at room temperature.

◆Sift together flour, baking power and soda.

◆Preheat oven to 340℉ (170℃ ) - 350℉ (180℃ ).

## Directions

① Cream the butter, and stir in sugar and salt. Beat well.

② Stir in beaten egg gradually, one - fourth at a time.

③ Fold in flour mixture and *okara*, then vanilla extract. Press the mixture together into a ball, and wrap in plastic wrap. Refrigerate at least 30 minutes.

④ Sandwich the dough between plastic wrap, and roll out to 1"-1 ¹/₂ " thickness. Remove top film and cut out shapes, dusting cookie cutter after each cutting. Refrigerate the dough if it becomes too soft to manage.

⑤ Place the cut-outs on a prepared baking tray, and bake at 340℉ (170℃ ) - 350℉ (180℃ ) for 15 minutes.

# Gem Breads

Introduced here is something between quiche and bread,
which can be a surprise for your guests.

Onion and Bacon Gems

Dried Tomato and Olive Gems

Difficulty Level ★★

Prep time: 25 minutes

## Dried Tomato and Olive Gems

### Ingredients

2¹/₂ oz (70 g)  unsalted chilled butter
5¹/₂ oz (150 g)  all purpose flour
A pinch of salt
1¹/₂ tsp  baking powder
1³/₄ oz (50 g)  granulated sugar
2  eggs, beaten with
    50 ml  soymilk
1³/₄ oz (50 g)  dried tomatoes,
    softened in
    2 Tbsp white wine
1³/₄ oz (50 g)  black olives, chopped

**(for 6" square tin)**

### Do-Ahead Tips

◆Chop and soak dried tomatoes
  in white wine for 2 hours.
◆Sift flour with salt, baking
  powder and sugar, and keep
  refrigerated until use.
◆Blend eggs with soymilk and
  keep refrigerated until use.
◆Preheat oven to 375℉(190℉ )-
  400℉(200℃ ).
◆Line baking tin with non-stick
  parchment.

### Directions

① Cut chilled butter into cubes
and add to the chilled flour
mixture. Rub butter into the
mixture. Rub between your
palms until the mixture
resembles fine breadcrumbs.

② Make a well in the middle, and into it pour the chilled egg mixture.
Blend well.
Add chopped dried tomatoes and olives, and blend well with a rubber
spatula so that no lump of flour is left.

③ Pour the mixture into
prepared baking tin, and smooth
top. Bake at 375℉(190℃)-400℉
(200℃) for 20 minutes, then
reduce heat to 340℉ (170℃)-
350℉ (180℃) and bake another
20 minutes.

## Onion and Bacon Gems

### Ingredients

2³/₄ oz (80 g)  unsalted butter
5¹/₂ oz (150 g)  all purpose
    flour, sifted with
    A pinch of salt
    1¹/₂ tsp  baking powder
    1³/₄ oz (50 g)
        granulated sugar
2  eggs, beaten with
    50 ml  soymilk
7 oz (200 g)  onion, sliced
3¹/₂ oz (100 g)  bacon, sliced
1 Tbsp (10 g)  butter for
    frying

**(for 7"/18 cm baking pan)**

### Do-Ahead Tips

◆Be sure to chill the
  dry ingredient
  mixture and egg
  mixture until use,
  just like Dried
  Tomato and Olive
  Bread (above).
◆Preheat oven to
  375℉(190℃)-400℉
  (200℃).
◆Line baking tin with
  non-stick parchment.

### Directions

①In a frying pan, melt
the butter for frying
and fry thinly sliced
onion and bacon over
high heat. When
moisture is released,
transfer to a shallow
pan to cool.

② Prepare dough as
Dried Tomato and
Olive Bread. Fold in
cooled onion and bacon.
Pour into prepared
baking pan and bake in
the same manner as
above.

# STEAMED/FRIED DESSERTS

Here are hearty desserts to be served warm on cooler days.

Green Tea Cupcake

Tomato Cupcake

Orange Cupcake

Difficulty Level ★★

Prep time: 25 minutes

# Steamed Cupcakes

**Colorful steamed cupcakes that are light and fluffy. Paper cups are trimmed to use as molds.**

## Ingredients

### Basic dough

1 egg
70 ml soymilk
1 Tbsp vegetable oil
¾ cup sugar
4¼ oz (120 g) all purpose flour
2 tsp baking powder

**(yields 6)**

### Tomato Cupcakes
Add: 3 Tbsp tomato puree
Mint sprigs

### Orange Cupcakes
Add: 100 ml orange juice
1 Tbsp grated orange
Orange rind

### Green Tea Cupcakes
Add: 2 tsp green tea powder
Glazed kidney beans or raisins

## Directions

### Tomato Cupcakes

① In a bowl, beat egg and sugar. Stir in tomato puree, soymilk, then vegetable oil.

② Sift together flour and baking powder, and add to the bowl. Pour into mold until 70 % full. Cook in a steamer for 15-20 minutes.

### Orange Cupcakes

Substitute tomato puree with orange juice and grated orange.

### Green Tea Cupcakes

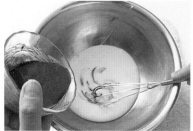 

① Do the same as Tomato Cupcakes, and divide batter into 2 portions. Add green tea to one portion and blend well.

② Pour ⅙ of the basic batter into a mold. Add green tea batter until 70 % full. Make marble pattern by stirring with a skewer.

# Ma Lai Koe

A famous Chinese steamed bread, here with chestnuts.
Place chestnuts during the steaming process to prevent sinking.

**Difficulty Level ★★**

**Prep time: 15 minutes**

## Ingredients

4¹/₂ oz (135 g) all purpose flour

¹/₄ lb each, brown sugar and plain sugar

3  eggs, beaten with
   1 egg yolk

40 ml  soymilk

1 tsp  soy sauce

75 ml  vegetable oil

1 Tbsp and ²/₃ tsp  baking soda

2 tsp  water

16  chestnuts in syrup (jarred)

**(yields 8)**

## Directions

① In a bowl, blend flour and brown sugar.

② Stir in beaten eggs and egg yolk. Beat until thickened, cover and rest in a refrigerator for about 1 hour.

③ Stir in soy sauce, vegetable oil and baking powder. Finally stir in baking soda.

④ Pour dough into 8 oblong baking pans lined with parchment. In a preheated steamer, steam for 7-8 minutes. Uncover to press chestnuts into top of each. Cover and steam for a further 15 minutes.

# Chinese Sesame Dumplings

**The popular, deep-fried dumpling with sweet bean jam, here featuring *tofu* in the dough for a milder flavor.**

> **Difficulty Level ★★**
>
> **Prep time: 30 minutes**

## Ingredients

1³/₄ oz (50 g)  soft *tofu*
1¹/₂ Tbsp  wheat starch
25 ml  boiling water
3 oz (85 g)  *shiratama-ko*, rice-flour for dumpling
50-55 ml  water
1 oz (30 g)  granulated sugar
1 Tsp  lard
3¹/₂ oz (100 g)  *adzuki* bean jam
White sesame seeds
Vegetable oil for deep-frying

**(yields 10)**

## Directions

① Wrap soft *tofu* in towel paper, and microwave for 1-1.5 minutes; drain. In a small bowl, place wheat starch, and add boiling water. Stir vigorously until well blended. Do not use cold water since hot water makes the viscosity needed for the dumpling.

② In a separate bowl, place *shiratama-ko*, *tofu*, and half of the cold water. Rub the mixture until it resembles coarse breadcrumbs.

③ Add sugar, lard and remaining water, and knead well until the dough is glossy and gathers into a lump.

④ On a floured surface, shape into a log, and cut into 10 pieces. Press each flat on your palm, and place small amount of bean jam. Gather sides to wrap up. Gently rub between your palms to form a ball. Make 10.

⑤ Coat with white sesame seeds all over. In 300℉(150℃) - 320℉ (160℃) oil, deep-fry

each dumpling, by resting each on a perforated spoon until it floats by itself, and pressing it under oil until plump and slightly golden. Drain and serve hot.

31

# Tofu Donuts

**Very stuffing, nutritious donuts with a hint of citrus scent.**

Difficulty Level ★

Prep time: 25 minutes

## Ingredients

1½ oz (40 g) unsalted butter

1¾ oz (50 g) granulated sugar

1¾ oz (50 g) *okara*\*

7 oz (200 g) all purpose flour, sifted with 2 tsp baking powder

Lemon rind of 1 lemon, grated

1 egg, beaten with 50 ml soymilk

Vegetable oil for deep-frying

Ground cinnamon

Granulated or icing sugar, for dusting

\*a by-product of *tofu*

**(yields 10-12)**

## Do-Ahead Tips

◆ Dice butter and chill 1 hour.

◆ Place sugar and *okara* in a bowl, and chill 1 hour.

## Directions

① In the bowl of sugar and *okara*, add flour mixture and grated lemon rind. Mix and add butter. Using a dough cutter or scraper, break butter into the mixture.

② Rub between palms until the mixture resembles breadcrumbs.

③ Make a well in the middle, and into it add egg mixture. Blend with surrounded flour mixture, and work into a ball. Wrap and chill for at least 30 minutes.

⑤ Deep-fry in medium-hot oil. To form a perfect center hole, gently twirl the ring by inserting a stick in the hole. Turn over several times until slightly brown. Let cool for 3 minutes and dust with sugar.

④ Sandwich dough between plastic wrap, and roll out into ³/₈" (1 cm) thickness. Cut out with a donut cutter.

**Fun-to-make yet tasty Spanish donut, here with *okara* for a crunchy texture.**

Difficulty Level ★★

Prep time: 25 minutes

### Ingredients

Vanilla churros

    100 ml  water

    $1\frac{1}{4}$ oz (50 g)  unsalted butter

    1 oz (30 g)  all purpose flour, sifted

    1 oz (30 g)  *okara**

    2-3  eggs, beaten well

    Vanilla extract

    Powdered sugar for dusting

    *a by-product of *tofu*

Chocolate churros

    Use the same ingredients as above, adding 1 Tbsp cocoa powder to the flour.

**(yields 10)**

### Do-Ahead Tips

◆Cut non-stick parchment into 7" by 2" (18 cm by 5 cm) rectangles.

### Directions

① In a saucepan heat the water and butter to a boil. Remove from heat and stir in sifted flour(add cocoa for chocolate churros) and *okara*. Blend well. Return to heat and cook for 1 minute stirring constantly. When a film is formed at the bottom of pan, remove from heat and transfer the batter to a bowl.

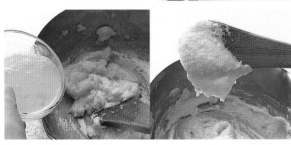

③ Using a piping bag with a star nozzle, pipe out the batter onto each parchment rectangle. In about 320℉(160℃) oil, deep-fry parchment side down, until golden brown. Let cool slightly and sprinkle with powdered sugar.

② Gradually add beaten eggs at 3-4 times, stirring after each addition. Stir until thickened enough to split when dropped some from spatula. Stir in vanilla extract.

# Tofu and Cheese Beignet

**The New Orleans French-style donut using soymilk.**

**Hot and fluffy beignets can be served either as an appetizer or dessert.**

Difficulty Level ★

Prep time: 20 minutes

## Ingredients

3½ Tbsp  granulated sugar

5½ oz (150 g)  all purpose flour,
   sifted with
     1 tsp baking powder

1  egg, beaten well

150 ml  soymilk

20  1" cubes natural cheese

**(yields 20)**

## Directions

① In a bowl mix sugar, flour mixture and *okara* until well blended.

② Make a well in the middle, and into it pour egg and soymilk. Whisk until smooth. Cover and chill at least for 30 minutes.

③ Coat each cheese cube with the batter, and deep-fry in 340°F (170°C) oil, dropping from an oil-coated teaspoon. Remove from oil when golden, and serve hot.

# French Toast with Soy Flour

**A delicious way to use day-old French bread. Try with *kinako*.**

**Difficulty Level ★**

**Prep time: 20 minutes**

## Ingredients

Egg mixture
  300ml soymilk
  $1/3$ stick vanilla bean
  2 eggs
  1 egg yolk
  $2^1/4$ oz (75 g) granulated
    sugar
$1/2$ loaf baguette
Butter for frying
$1/2$ cup *kinako*, soy flour
Molasses for topping

**(serves 4)**

## Do-Ahead Tips

◆Preheat oven to
400℉ (200℃).

◆Make egg mixture by
blending all the
ingredients well and
pass through a
strainer.

## Directions

① Cut baguette into bite-size
pieces. Dip them in egg mixture
briefly.

② In heated butter, fry dipped
bread pieces over medium heat
until golden.

③ Transfer bread pieces to a
prepared baking sheet, and bake
at 400℉ (200℃) for 8 minutes.
Arrange on a serving dish, and
serve with soy flour and
molasses.

# FRUIT DESSERTS

**A dessert with seasonal fruits makes a perfect ending for any meal.**

Difficulty Level ★★★

Prep time: 30 minutes

# Cherry Tart

**Sweet and sour cherry filling wrapped in short crust is everyone's favorite.**

## Ingredients

Tart dough:
3¼ oz (90 g)  unsalted
   butter
5 Tbsp  granulated sugar
½ egg, beaten
1 Tbsp  soymilk
Vanilla oil
1 cup and 1 Tbsp  all
   purpose flour
½ tsp  baking powder
1 ½ Tbsp ground almonds

Filling:
1 lb (450 g)  fresh
   cherries
3 Tbsp  unsalted butter
3 Tbsp  granulated sugar
2 Tbsp  lemon juice
2 Tbsp  cornstarch
½ tsp  cinnamon
1 Tbsp  kirsch
Powdered sugar, for
   dusting

**(for 7" tart pan)**

### Do-Ahead Tips

◆Shift together
   flour, baking
   powder and
   almond powder.
◆Preheat oven to
   350℉ (180℃).

## Directions

① Stone cherries by slitting into each, or using a cherry stoner.

② Melt butter in a frying pan, and saute cherries with sugar just until coated with butter. Add all remaining ingredients and keep stirring until the moisture evaporates.

③ Transfer into a shallow baking pan, and set aside to cool.

④ Prepare tart dough. In a bowl, cream the butter, and add sugar. Stir in beaten egg gradually.

⑤ Add sifted flour mixture, soymilk and vanilla oil, and mix well. Press into a ball, and wrap in a plastic wrap. Refrigerate for an hour.

⑥ Lay plastic wrap under and over the dough, and roll out into ¹/₁₆" thickness.

⑦ Removing the plastic wrap, line a tart pan with the dough so that it runs over the edges. Chill whenever it feels sticky as you work.

⑧ Place the cooled filling into the prepared tart. Fold the dough over the filling, making pleats.
Bake at 350℉ (180℃) for 25 - 30 minutes. Remove from the oven, and let cool in the pan. Sift with powdered sugar.

# Citus Cupcakes

**Refreshing, citrus flavored cupcakes, irresistible with a dash of cream.**

Difficulty Level ★★

Prep time: 25 minutes

## Ingredients

2 large eggs, at room
temperature
3 oz (85 g)  granulated sugar
2¼ oz (60 g)  unsalted butter
2 tsp  soymilk
1  *yuzu* or ½ lemon, squeezed
2 tsp  grated *yuzu* or lemon rind
3½ oz (100 g)  all purpose
flour, sifted
½ cup  heavy/whipping cream
2 Tbsp  soymilk
Citrus rind

### (for 6  3" muffin pans)

## Do-Ahead Tips

◆Butter pans, and
line with paper
cups.
◆Preheat oven to
340℉ (170℃).

## Directions

① In a bowl, beat eggs and add granulated sugar.
Whisk over a bowl of hot water, about 140℉ (60℃),
until thick enough to hold a trail in a clear ribbon.
In a separate bowl, melt butter over hot water. Stir
in soymilk, citric juice and grated citrus rind.

② Fold in sifted flour. When some of the flour is
still visible, whirl in butter mixture and combine
briefly. Pour into lined muffin pans, and bake at
340℉ (170℃) for 20 minutes.

③ Scoop out centers of
each cake; cut away
thick part, and cut into
halves.

④ Whip cream with
soymilk, and pipe into
the hollow of each cake.
Decorate with sponge
pieces and citrus rind.

# Baked Apple Custard

**A quick-to-prepare, yet flavorful custard pudding with tart apple and *tofu* crumble.**

Difficulty Level ★

Prep time: 15 minutes

## Ingredients

1 cup soymilk
1 large egg
1 egg yolk
3 oz (85 g) granulated
  sugar
1¹/₂ Tbsp all purpose flour
1¹/₂ Tbsp ground almonds
¹/₄ cup heavy/whipping
  cream
¹/₄ cup white wine
2 cooking apples, sliced
Granulated sugar, for
  dusting
*Tofu* Crumble (Page 13)

**(for 6 4" tart pans)**

## Do-Ahead Tips

◆Sift together flour
  and ground almonds.
◆Make *Tofu* crumble.
◆Preheat oven to
  340℉ (170℃) - 350℉
  (180℃).

## Directions

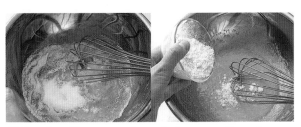

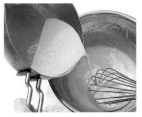

① In a saucepan, heat soymilk just until it starts to boil.

② In a bowl beat together whole egg, yolk and granulated sugar. Stir in flour mixture and blend well.

③ When the mixture becomes smooth, add soymilk, cream and wine. Blend well.

④ Arrange thinly sliced apple in each tartlet dish. Pour over custard mixture.

⑤ Place dishes in baking pan. Fill the pan with hot water, and bake for about 15 minutes. Let cool, and sprinkle with granulated sugar. Let stand for a further 20 to 25 minutes before serving.

# Pancake Tower

**Petite pancakes layered with berries and cream to form a tall, fun dessert.**

Difficulty Level ★

Prep time: 20 minutes

## Ingredients

7 oz (200 g)  all purpose
   flour
2 tsp  baking powder
2 Tbsp  sugar
$\frac{1}{2}$ tsp  salt
300 ml  soymilk
1  egg, beaten
1 Tbsp  vegetable oil,
   mixed with
   1 Tbsp honey
Raspberries, blueberries,
   red currants, banana,
   etc.
Whipping cream
Soymilk custard
Mint sprigs

**( yields 4)**

## Do-Ahead Tips

◆Sift together flour
   and baking powder.

## Directions

① In a bowl, mix flour
and baking powder.
Stir in sugar and salt.
Make a well in the
middle.

② Blend soymilk and
egg, and pour into the
well. Whisk until
smooth.

③ Stir in vegetable oil
mixture. Cover and
chill for half an hour.

④ Heat non-stick frying pan. Add the batter. When
small bubbles float, turn over and cook until
golden. Make a dozen tiny pancakes.

⑤ Lay a pancake. Pipe
out soymilk custard.
Arrange fruits. Pipe out
whipped cream. Repeat
and end with whipped
cream and fruit.

# Fruit Gratin

**Originally a French "batter" pudding, this berry clafoutis uses soymilk for a more delicate flavor.**

> Difficulty Level ★
>
> Prep time: 15 minutes

## Ingredients

250 ml  soymilk
1  egg, beaten with
   1 egg yolk
2 ½ oz (70 g)  granulated sugar
2 tsp  all purpose flour
1 Tbsp  ground almond
50 ml  heavy / whipping cream
5 oz (149 g)  mixed berries e.g.
   blackberries, raspberries,
   blueberries, gooseberries,
   redcurrants, etc.
Granulated sugar for dusting

**(serves 4)**

## Do-Ahead Tips

◆ Preheat the oven to 350℉ (180℃).
◆ Sift together flour and ground almonds.

## Directions

① In a saucepan heat soymilk just until it starts bubbling, and remove from heat.
In a bowl, beat egg mixture and granulated sugar.

② Stir in flour mixture. Add only 2 tablespoons soymilk, and blend well until creamy.

③ Stir in remaining soymilk and cream.

④ In an oven-proof serving dish, arrange the berries. Pour the batter over them. Add some more berries to display.
Place on baking tray, and fill the tray with hot water. Bake at 340℉ (170℃) - 350℉(180℃) for 20-25 minutes until risen. Sprinkle with granulated sugar just before serving.

# Cranberry Bread

**Lovely in flavor and color, this not-so-sweet bread can be a good accompaniment to meals.**

## Ingredients

2¹/₂ oz (70 g) unsalted butter, chilled

2 eggs, blended with

   70 ml soymilk

   1 Tbsp honey

5¹/₂ oz (150 g) all purpose flour

A pinch of salt

1¹/₂ tsp baking powder

1¹/₄ oz (50 g) granulated sugar

3 oz (80 g) dried cranberries

**(for 7" x 3¹/₄ " x 2¹/₂ "**

**(18x8x6 cm) baking tin)**

**Difficulty Level ★★**

**Prep time: 20 minutes**

## Do-Ahead Tips

◆ Blend eggs, soymilk and honey; chill.

◆ Sift together flour and baking powder. Blend with salt and sugar; chill the mixture.

◆ Preheat oven to 375℉(190℃) - 400℉(200℃).

## Directions

① Soften dried cranberries in warm water, and drain.

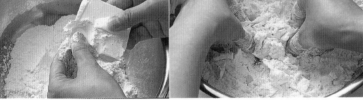

② Tear chilled butter and blend into chilled dry ingredients. Press butter chunks with your fingers.

③ Rub between palms until the mixture resembles fine breadcrumbs.

④ Make a well in the middle, and into it pour the egg mixture. Blend well.

⑤ Fold in softened cranberries. Pour the mixture into prepared baking tin, and bake at 375℉(190℃) - 400℉(200℃) for 20 minutes. Reduce heat to 340℉(170℃)-350℉(170℃) and bake another 20 minutes.

**Fragrant and flavorful cake with lots of bananas, sour cream and soymilk.**

Difficulty Level ★★

Prep time: 30 minutes

## Ingredients

$2^3/4$ oz (80 g)  unsalted butter

1 oz (30 g)  sour cream

$3^1/2$ oz (100 g)  powdered sugar

2  eggs, beaten

30 ml  soymilk

A pinch of salt

$5^1/2$ oz (150 g)  all purpose flour,
  sifted with
   $^2/3$ tsp  baking powder

$1^1/2$ oz (40 g)  coconut powder

2 ripe bananas

$1^3/4$ oz (50 g)  apricot jelly, thinned
  with
  1 Tbsp hot water

Shredded coconut, toasted

### (for 6" square tin)

### Do-Ahead Tips

◆Preheat oven to 340°F (170°C) -
  350°F (180°C).

◆Line baking tin with non-stick
  parchment.

## Directions

① In a bowl beat butter and sour
cream until smooth. Add
powdered sugar and blend well.

② Stir in beaten eggs gradually,
then add soymilk. If the mixture
is separated, sprinkle with 1
Tbsp of the flour mixture and
blend well.

③ Stir in salt. Add sifted flour
mixture and coconut powder.
Blend well using a rubber
spatula.

④ In the prepared baking pan,
pour half amount of the dough.
Slice bananas into $^3/8$" (1 cm)
rounds and arrange on the
dough. Pour in remaining dough,
flatten the top and bake at 340°F
(170°C) - 350°F (180°C) for 30-35
minutes.

⑤ Remove from the pan and
brush with thinned apricot jam.
Top with toasted coconut.

# Fruit and Bread Pudding

**An unbeatable favorite for wintry days.**

Difficulty Level ★

Prep time: 15 minutes

## Ingredients

$^1/_2$ baguette
2 plums, quartered
$1^1/_2$ oz (40 g) raisins
200 ml soymilk
100ml heavy/whipping cream
$^1/_4$ stick vanilla bean
$2^1/_4$ oz (60 g) granulated sugar
3 eggs, beaten
1 Tbsp rum
*Tofu* Crumble
   $1^1/_2$ oz (40 g) unsalted butte
   $1^1/_2$ oz (40 g) granulated sugar
   1 oz (30 g) *okara**,
   $^1/_3$ oz (10 g) ground almonds
   $^3/_4$ oz (20 g) all purpose flour
   *a by-product of *tofu*

### ( for 7-8 $2^3/_4$" ramekins)

## Do-Ahead Tips

◆Prepare *Tofu* Crumble referring to page 13.
◆Preheat oven to 350℉ (180℃).
◆Grease ramekins with extra butter.

## Directions

① Cut baguette into bite-size pieces. Place them in buttered ramekins.
Place plums in the ramekins. Sprinkle with raisins.

② In a saucepan, heat soymilk, cream, vanilla bean and sugar. Remove from heat just before boiling.

③ Into beaten eggs, add soymilk mixture gradually, whisking well after each addition.
Pass through a strainer, and stir in rum.

④ Pour into the ramekins. Sprinkle with *Tofu* Crumble, and bake at 350℉ (180℃) for 20-25 minutes. If a toothpick inserted in the center comes out clean, remove from the oven.

**A juicy apple compote, baked with *tofu* crumble. Serve piping hot.**

## Ingredients

3  cooking apples
$^1/_2$  lemon, sliced
800 ml  water
$^1/_3$  stick vanilla bean
1  cinnamon stick
*Tofu* Crumble
   $1^1/_2$ oz (40 g)  unsalted
    butter
   1 oz (30 g)  *okara**
   $^1/_3$ oz (10 g)  ground
    almonds
   $^3/_4$ oz (20 g)  all purpose
    flour
   $1^1/_2$ oz (40 g)
    granulated sugar
   Cinnamon powder
*a by-product of *tofu*

**(serves 6)**

## Do-Ahead Tips

◆Preheat oven to
350°F (180°C) - 375°F
(190°C) .

## Directions

① Cut apples vertically in halves, peel and remove cores. Soak apples in the water with lemon slices for 10 minutes.

② In a saucepan, place drained apples. Add granuled sugar and 700ml of the soaking water. Cook over medium low heat. Cover with a round cut parchment, with a center hole to release steam. When the sugar dissolves, reduce heat and simmer for about 25 minutes until $^2/_3$ of the apples are transparent. (Turn over once.)

③ Transfer apples to a bowl, and set aside. Remove floating bubbles from the saucepan, and add the remaining soaking water. Turn heat high and bring to a boil. Pour over the apples, add cinnamon stick and vanilla bean.
Make *Tofu* Crumble referring to page 13.

④ Place apple in an ovenproof serving dish. Sprinkle with *Tofu* Crumble, and bake at 350°F (180°C) - 375°F (190°C) for 10-12 minutes. Serve hot.

# CHILLED DESSERTS

Here are all popular cold desserts from *tofu* ice cream to fluffy green-tea mousse featuring *tofu* or *tonyu* (soymilk).

## Mango Mousse

**Fluffy tropical mousse with mango chunks, inspired from the popular Chinese dessert.**

Difficulty Level ★★

Prep time: 25 minutes

### Ingredients

1 Tbsp (10 g)  gelatin powder,
4  fresh mangoes, diced
1³/₄ oz (50 g)  granulated sugar
180 ml  water
200 ml  soymilk
65 ml  heavy/whipping cream
¹/₂  mango, for topping

**(serves 4)**

### Directions

① Soak the gelatin powder in 3 Tbsp water (extra) for 3-5 minutes.

② Puree half of the diced 2 mangoes in a food processor.

⑤ Transfer into a bowl over ice water. Stir and cool slightly. Drizzle in soymilk and cream. Stir well until slightly thickened. Add remaining mango chunks and stir gently.
Pour into a shallow mold and chill until set. Arrange on individual dish and add  mango chunks for topping.

③ In a saucepan heat sugar and the water. Add mango puree.

④ Bring to a boil once, and turn off heat. Add softened gelatin, and stir until dissolved.

# Blancmange

**Blancmange is an almond-flavored cooked cream and flummery.
Here is a chilled version with fresh and colorful fruits.**

Difficulty Level ★★

Prep time: 20 minutes

## Ingredients

4 tsp (13 g) gelatin
    powder
3¹/₂ oz (100 g) sliced
    almonds
300ml soymilk
Sugar syrup
  200 ml water
  4 oz (110 g) granulated
    sugar
200 ml heavy/whipping
  cream
Fresh seasonal fruits
Whipped cream
  60 ml heavy/whipping
  cream
  1 tsp granulated sugar

**(serves 5-6)**

## Do-Ahead Tips

◆Soak gelatin powder
in 4 Tbsp water
(extra) for 3-5
minutes.
◆Make sugar syrup by
boiling down the
water and sugar.

## Directions

① In a frying pan roast
sliced almonds over low
heat, tilting the pan
constantly until a nutty
aroma is released.

② In a saucepan heat
soymilk and the
almonds. Cook over low
heat for 5-6 minutes.
Stir in softened gelatin.

⑥ Pour into individual
mold and chill for 1
hour until set. Unmold
and arrange fruits of
your choice. Pour
lightly whipped cream.

③ Add sugar syrup to
the soymilk mixture,
and pass through a
strainer.

④ Transfer to a bowl
over ice water to
thicken.

⑤ In a separate bowl,
whip cream until
slightly thickened, and
fold it into the mixture.

# Creme Brulee

**Enjoy an irresistible harmony between the somewhat bitter, crisp caramelized glaze and the creamy custard.**

**Difficulty Level ★**

**Prep time: 15 minutes**

### Ingredients

4  egg yolks
300 ml  heavy/whipping
   cream
200 ml  soymilk
2³/₄ oz (75 g)  granulated
   sugar
1  stick vanilla bean
Granulated or brown
   sugar for topping

**(yields 7-8  3¹/₄"-
3¹/₂" ramekins)**

### Do-Ahead Tips

◆Separate vanilla
  bean into pod and
  beans.
◆Preheat oven to
  275℉(140℃)-300℉
  (150℃).

## Directions

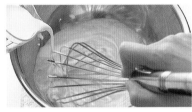

① In a bowl, stir egg yolks and
heavy/whipping cream.

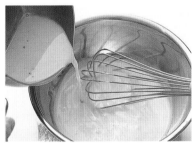

② In a small saucepan, heat
soymilk, sugar and vanilla beans
and pod. When it almost reaches
the boiling point, remove from
heat and pour into the egg yolk
mixture. Stir well.

③ Pour into individual ramekins,
and place them in a shallow baking
pan. Pour some water into the pan
and bake at 275℉(140℃)-300℉
(150℃) for 20-25 minutes.

④ When cooled, top the custard
with a thick layer of sugar. Using
a gas burner (for outdoor use) or
putting under a hot grill, melt the
sugar until caramelized. Chill
until the custard is set again and
topping becomes crisp.

**A Japanese version of Bavarian Cream.**

**Difficulty Level ★★**

**Prep time: 20 minutes**

## Ingredients

1 Tbsp (10 g)  gelatin
powder, softened in 3
Tbsp water

300 ml  soymilk

1/2 stick  vanilla bean

3  egg yolks

2 3/4 oz (80 g)  granulated
sugar

3 1/2 oz (100 g)  soft *tofu*

200 ml  heavy/whipping
cream

1 Tbsp  Grand Manier

Grapefruit

Mint sprigs

Molasses

**(yields 6 )**

## Do-Ahead Tips

◆Wrap *tofu* in a
kitchen towel and
microwave for 1
minute 30 seconds;
drain.

◆Soak gelatin powder
in 3 Tbsp water
(extra) for 3-5
minutes.

## Directions

① In a small saucepan,
heat soymilk, sugar,
vanilla beans and pod.
When it almost reaches
the boiling point,
remove from heat.

② In a bowl, beat egg
yolks and add
granulated sugar. Beat
until pale. Add soymilk
mixture gradually,
stirring constantly.

③ Pass the mixture
through a strainer into
the saucepan. Cook and
stir over low heat until
a spatula rubbed with a
finger holds its trail.

④ Remove from heat and add softened gelatin. Stir
well, and pass through strainer. Stir in *tofu*.

⑤ In a separate bowl,
whip cream with Grand
Marnier until slightly
thickened.

⑥ Pour into individual
molds and chill for 1
hour until set.
Unmold and serve
accompanied with
grapefruit segments
and mint sprigs. Pour
over molasses.

# Kinako Tiramisu

*Kinako*, **or soy flour, has a delicate flavor enhanced when mixed with sugar.**
**Thinned molasses is used to replace espresso syrup.**

Difficulty Level ★

Prep time: 25 minutes

## Ingredients

2 ⅔ tsp (8 g)  gelatin powder

3  egg yolks

2¼ oz (60 g)  granulated sugar

1 Tbsp  *kinako*, soy flour
  2 tsp  superfine sugar

1¾ oz (50 g)  mascarpone

250 ml  soymilk

1 Tbsp  kirsh

80 ml  heavy/whipping cream,lightly whipped

Shop-bought sponge

3 Tbsp  molasses

 3 Tbsp water

Topping

  80 ml  heavy/whipping cream,lightly whipped with

   1 tsp  granulated sugar

*Kinako*, soy flour for dusting

Chunky *adzuki* bean jam

## (serves 6-7)

## Directions

① Soak gelatin in 3 Tbsp water (extra) for 3-5 minutes.

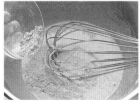

② In a bowl, beat egg yolks and sugar. Mix *kinako* and sugar, and add to the bowl.

③ Stir well until pale. Stir in mascarpone cheese.

④ In a small saucepan, heat soymilk and remove from heat just before boiling. Stir in softened gelatin. When the gelatin is completely dissolved, gradually add to the bowl. Also add kirsh. Place the bowl over ice water, and stir until thickened.

⑤ Fold whipped cream into the batter, half amount at a time.

⑥ Line a mold with sliced sponge. Brush on molasses thinned with water.

⑦ Pour in the batter. Place another layer of sponge, and brush with thinned molasses. Repeat this to fill the mold.

⑧ Pour whipped cream over the sponge. Chill at least 1 hour. Slice and serve with *adzuki* bean jam, and sprinlke with *kinako*.

# Lemon Ginger Jelly

**A refreshing, chilled jelly is always a popular way of ending a meal. Here, tangy jelly is enhanced with milk cream pudding.**

**Difficulty Level ★★**

**Prep time: 50 minutes**

## Ingredients

Soymilk Pudding
- 3 tsp (9 g)  gelatin leaf or powder
- 300 ml  soymilk
- 1¾ oz (50 g)  granulated sugar
- 50 ml  heavy/whipping cream

Lemon Ginger Jelly
- 2 tsp (6 g)  gelatin powder
- 300 ml  ginger ale
- 2 Tbsp  lemon juice
- 50 ml  water
- 2 tsp  ginger juice
- ¾  slices fresh gingerroot

Decoration
- Melon, scooped into balls
- Lemon, sliced
- Lemon balm leaves

**(yields 4 )**

## Do-Ahead Tips

◆ Soak gelatin in water (extra) to soften.

◆ Wash gingerroot well under running water, and slice unpeeled.

## Directions

① In a saucepan heat together soymilk and sugar. When the sugar is dissolved, turn off heat just before reaching the boiling point. Stir in lightly squeezed gelatin.

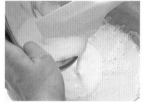

② Transfer to a bowl over ice water, and beat until slightly thickened. Whip heavy/whipping cream lightly and stir into the mixture.

③ Spoon the mixture into individual glasses, and chill.

④ In a clean saucepan, heat ginger ale, lemon juice with granulated sugar until the sugar dissolves. Remove from heat before reaching the boiling point, and stir in softened gelatin powder, then ginger slices and juice.

⑤ Once cooled, pour into the glass of milk pudding. Arrange melon bowls and a slice of lemon. Chill until set, and serve with a lemon balm leaf.

# Fruit Jelly with Tofu Creme Anglaise

**A clear jelly tower, served with *tofu* creme Anglaise.**

**Difficulty Level ★**

**Prep time: 45 minutes**

## Ingredients

3(¹/₄ oz/10 g) gelatin leaves
250 ml  water
1¹/₂ oz (40 g)  granulated sugar
¹/₂ Tbsp  lemon juice
40 ml  white wine
1  dozen raspberries
1  dozen blueberries
2¹/₄ oz (60 g)  orange segments
3  slices canned pineapple
*Tofu* Creme Anglaise (below)

## (for 5 custard cups)

## Do-Ahead Tips

◆Soak gelatin leaves in ample water (extra) for 3-5 minutes.
◆Make Creme Anglaise.
◆Cut orange and pineapple into chunks.

## Directions

① In a saucepan heat water, granulated sugar, lemon juice and white wine until the sugar dissolves. Turn off heat before reaching the boiling point. Stir in lightly squeezed gelatin leaves.

④ Unmold and serve with *Tofu* Creme Anglaise.

② Transfer to a bowl over ice water, and let cool. Add fruits and stir gently until slightly thickened.

### Creme Anglaise

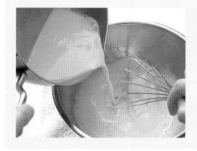

③ Pour into individual custard cups and chill for 1 hour until set.

In a bowl beat together 2 egg yolks and 1³/₄ oz (50 g) granulated sugar. Gradually add in warmed soymilk, stirring constantly. Transfer to a saucepan and cook over low heat until thickened. Remove from heat and let cool over ice water.

# Yogurt Mousse

**A refreshing dessert, combining sweet mango and sour yogurt.**

## Ingredients (for 7"/18 cm baking pan)

1  slice shop-bought sponge
Yogurt mousse
   2 2/3 tsp (8 g)  gelatin powder
   200 ml  soymilk
   3 1/2 oz (100 g)  plain yogurt
   150 ml  heavy/whipping cream
   2 3/4 oz (80 g)  granulated sugar
   2  egg yolks

White wine jelly
   1/2 Tbsp (5 g)  gelatin powder,
      soaked in 1 Tbsp water
   1 1/2 oz (40 g)  granulated sugar
   100 ml  water
   4 Tbsp  white wine
   2 tsp  lemon juice
1 1/2  fresh mangoes, sliced
Red currants

**Difficulty Level ★★**

**Prep time: 1 hour**

## Do-Ahead Tips

◆ Soak gelatin separately in triple amount of water for 3-5 minutes.

## Directions

① Cut sponge to the size of mold, and line the bottom of it.

② In a saucepan, heat soymilk, yogurt, cream and half amount of the sugar. Cook and stir until the sugar dissolves. While hot, stir in softened gelatin. Stir well.

③ In a bowl, beat egg yolk with remaining sugar until pale and creamy. Stir in soymilk mixture gradually. Place the bowl over ice water, and keep stirring until slightly thickened and fluffy.

④ Pour over the sponge, and chill for 30 minutes.

⑤ Make white wine jelly. Soak gelatin triple amount of water (extra).
In a saucepan heat sugar, wine and lemon juice until the sugar dissolves. While hot, add softened gelatin, and stir until completely dissolved.

⑥ When cooled, arrange sliced mango and red currants. Pour in white wine jelly mixture. Chill at least 40-50 minutes.

⑦ Unmold by wrapping the mold with a hot steamed towel.

55

# Coffee Cheesecake

*Tofu* is used to reduce the cheese in this bittersweet cheesecake.

## Ingredients

Crust
  2$^1/_4$ oz (60 g)  graham crackers
  1$^1/_2$ oz (40 g)  unsalted butter, at
    room temperature
Filling
  2$^3/_4$ oz (80 g)  cream cheese, at
    room temperature
  1$^1/_2$ oz (40 g)  unsalted butter, at
    room temperature
  2$^3/_4$ oz (80 g)  granulated sugar
  1 oz (30 g)  sour cream

3$^1/_2$ oz (100 g)  soft *tofu*, drained
2 tsp  lemon juice
1$^1/_2$ Tbsp instant coffee granules,
    dissolved in same amount of water
1 Tbsp  coffee liqueur
2 tsp (6 g)  gelatin powder
Whipped cream
Sliced almonds
Cocoa powder
**(for 6"/15 cm square pan)**

Difficulty Level ★★

Prep time: 30 minutes

## Directions

① Make crust. Break graham crackers using a rolling pin. Microwave butter to soften and mix with the crackers.

### Do-Ahead Tips

◆Soak gelatin powder in 1$^1/_2$ Tbsp water (extra) for 3-5 minutes.

② Press the graham cracker mixture on the bottom of mold.

③ Make filling. In a bowl, whisk cream cheese and butter until smooth. Add sugar and stir well, then sour cream, and *tofu*. Add lemon juice, dissolved coffee and coffee liqueur. Blend well.

④ Transfer $^1/_3$ amount of the mixture into a separate bowl over hot water. Stir in softened gelatin. When gelatin is dissolved, add to the remaining mixture and blend well.

⑤ In another bowl, whip cream until thickened. Fold it into the mixture evenly.

⑥ Pour into the mold, and chill for 30 minutes until set. Slice and decorate with whipped cream. Sprinkle with toasted sliced almonds and cocoa powder.

# Creme de Anjou

This *tofu* cheese mousse has sweet and sour berry sauce inside, and Creme Anglaise around it.

## Ingredients

2 3/4 oz (80 g) egg white
1 oz (30 g) granulated sugar
Sugar syrup
   1 1/4 oz (35 g) granulated sugar
   15 ml water
3 1/2 oz (100 g) soft *tofu*
7 oz (200 g) cream cheese
100 ml heavy/whipping cream
Berry Sauce
   4 fresh strawberries
   1 1/2 oz (40 g) fresh or frozen
    raspberries

1 oz (25 g) fresh or frozen
  blueberries
1/2 oz (15 g) granulated sugar
1 tsp lemon juice
1 1/2 tsp cornstarch, dissolved in
  1 1/2 tsp water
*Tofu* Creme Anglaise
  2 egg yolks
  50 ml granulated sugar
  220 ml soymilk

**(yields 6)**

Difficulty Level ★★

Prep time: 50 minutes

## Do-Ahead Tips

◆ Chill egg whites in a steel bowl.
◆ Wrap *tofu* in kitchen towel and microwave for 1-1.5 minutes; let stand to drain.
◆ Make Creme Anglaise.

## Directions

① Make berry sauce. Heat all Berry Sauce ingredients, omitting cornstarch solution, covered, for 7-8 minutes over low heat. Remove from heat and stir in dissolved cornstarch. Return to heat and cook until thickened. Transfer to a shallow baking pan, and let cool.

② Make mousse. Whip egg whites until thickened but still runny. Add granulated sugar and whip again until soft peaks form.

③ In a small saucepan, boil down sugar syrup ingredients to reach 242℉ (117℃), until water drops form tiny pearls.

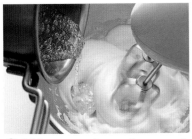

④ Add syrup to the meringue, and whip until glossy. Chill until use.

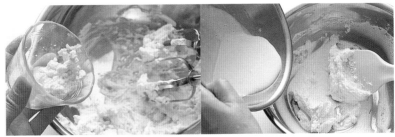

⑤ In a separate bowl, beat together drained *tofu* and cream cheese. Stir in lightly whipped cream.

⑥ Fold meringue into cheese mixture, half amount at a time.

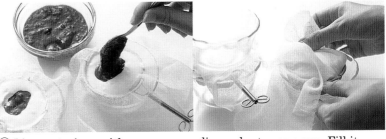

⑦ Line a strainer with gauze or muslin, and set over a cup. Fill it with the mousse ²/₃ full. Spoon the center out, and fill it with berry sauce. Cover it with mouse, and wrap up with gauze or muslin. Top with a weight and chill for 1-3 hours until set.

⑧ Unwrap and place in a "pool" of Creme Anglaise.

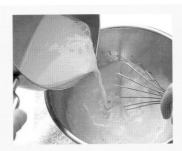

### Cream Anglaise

In a bowl, beat together egg yolks and sugar. Gradually stir in warmed soymilk. Transfer to a saucepan and heat until thickened over low heat. Remove from heat and let cool over ice water.

# Watermelon Jelly

Enjoy the harmony of sweet watermelon jelly and rich milk pudding.

Difficulty Level ★★

Prep time: 50 minutes

## Ingredients

Watermelon Jelly
  3 tsp (9 g)  gelatin powder,
  350 ml  watermelon juice
Soymilk Pudding
  3 tsp (9 g)  gelatin powder
  350 ml  soymilk
  1³/₄ oz (50 g)  granulated sugar
  20 ml  sour cream
  70 ml  heavy/whipping cream

**( yields 4-5)**

## Directions

① Make soymilk pudding. In a saucepan heat soymilk and sugar until the sugar dissolves. Turn off heat just before the boiling.

② While hot, add softened gelatin powder. Stir well, and add sour cream.

④ In a separate bowl, whip heavy/whipping cream until thickened. Stir in a small amount of soymilk mixture, then add the remaining, and blend well.
Pour into individual serving glasses, and chill until almost set.

## Do-Ahead Tips

◆Soak each amount of gelatin powder separately in 2 Tbsp water (extra) for 3-5 minutes.
◆Remove pips from watermelon and puree in a food processor. Strain to make juice.

③ Transfer to a bowl, and stir over ice water until slightly thickened.

⑤ Make watermelon jelly. In a small saucepan, boil down 1/3 amount of watermelon juice for about 3 minutes, and stir in softened gelatin,and then the remaining juice.
Pour over milk pudding and chill for 50-60 minutes.

# Orange Jelly Version

## Ingredients

2 ¹/₂ tsp (8 g) gelatin powder
350 ml orange juice
1 ¹/₄ oz (35 g) granulated sugar
2 tsp kirsch

## Directions

① Soak gelatin powder in 1 Tbsp water (extra) until softened. Make soymilk pudding.
② In a saucepan, heat orange juice and granulated sugar. Stir until sugar dissolves, and remove from heat just before boiling.
③ Stir in softened gelatin. Pass through a strainer, and add kirsch. Let cool.
④ When the soymilk pudding begins to set, pour in orange jelly liquid. Chill for 40-50 minutes.

# Tofu Ice Creams

**Refreshing *tofu* ice cream made at home makes a perfect dessert after any kind of meal.**

## Vanilla Ice Cream

### Ingredients

500 ml  soymilk
$^1/_4$  stick vanilla bean
6  egg yolks
$5^1/_2$ oz (150 g)  granulated sugar
$^3/_4$ oz (20 g)  skimmed milk powder
200 ml  heavy/ whipping cream

**(serves 4-6)**

### Do-Ahead Tips

◆Combine granulated sugar and skimmed milk powder.

### Directions

① Split vanilla bean and scrape out beans. Add to a saucepan filled with soymilk, and heat just until it starts to bubble. Cover and let stand for 30 minutes.

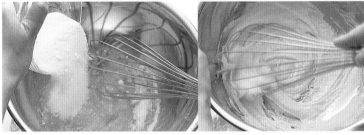

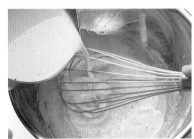

② In a bowl, beat together egg yolks and sugar mixture until pale and creamy.

③ Add soymilk gradually, stirring constantly. Stir in heavy/whipping cream.

④ Transfer to a saucepan, and cook slowly until slightly thickened. Remove from heat if the mixture on a wooden spatula stays still when you run your finger. Strain through Chinois or fine sieve and cool over ice water. Transfer to a shallow metal container, and chill for 5 hours until it begins to freeze.

⑤ Using an electric beater, incorporate air by whisking. Chill again for 1 hour. Whisk again; chill. Repeat this 2 times.

## Chocolate Ice Cream

### Ingredients

500 ml  soymilk
$2^1/_4$ oz (60 g)  baker's sweet chocolate
6  egg yolks
$5^1/_2$ oz (150 g)  granulated sugar
$^3/_4$ oz (20 g)  skimmed milk powder
200 ml  heavy/ whipping cream

**(serves 4-6 )**

### Do-Ahead Tips

◆Combine granulated sugar and skimmed milk powder.

### Directions

① In a saucepan heat soymilk until hot, but do not boil. In a bowl over simmering water, melt chocolate, stirring constantly. In separate bowl, beat together egg yolks and sugar mixture until pale and creamy. Add soymilk and mix well. Stir in heavy/whipping cream.

② Transfer it to the saucepan, and cook over medium low heat stirring constantly until thickened. Pass through a fine strainer such as Chinois and blend with melted chocolate.

# Parfait Japanesque

**An assortment of *tofu* ice cream, green tea cream and *adzuki* bean jam.**

Difficulty Level ★

Prep time: 20 minutes

## Ingredients

4 scoops *tofu* ice cream ( page 63)
1¹/₂ oz (40 g)  *shiratama-ko*\*
120 ml  heavy/whipping cream
2 tsp  powdered green tea
2 tsp  granulated sugar
3¹/₂ oz (100 g)  *adzuki* bean jam
Yellow peach, canned
Cherries

\*rice flour for dumpling

**(serves 4)**

## Directions

① Blend rice flour with
appropriate amount water (see
package) and knead until as soft
as an earlobe. Form into balls
and cook in boiling water.
Remove when they float to the
surface.

② In a bowl, beat together
heavy/whipping cream,
powdered green tea and sugar
until stiff.

③ In a serving dish, place a scoop
of ice cream. Pipe out green tea
cream, and arrange rice-flour
dumpling, bean jam and fruits.

# Chocolate Trifle

**Chocolate *tofu* ice cream teamed with fruits and almonds.**

Difficulty Level ★★

Prep time: 20 minutes

## Ingredients

4 scoops choc *tofu* ice cream

120 ml heavy/whipping cream

2 tsp granulated sugar

Lady's fingers

Sliced almonds, toasted

Fruits (cherry, orange, peach, etc)

Mint sprigs

**(serves 4)**

## Directions

① In a bowl over ice water, whip heavy/whipping cream with granulated sugar until thickened.

② Break lady's fingers into a serving glass. Place scooped *tofu* ice cream on it.

③ Spoon in whipped cream. Layer fruits. Layer *tofu* ice cream. Arrange some fruits, and decorate with toasted sliced almonds and mint sprigs.

# Kanten Jelly Duo

Enjoy the slippery, smooth texture of *kanten* as well as the contrast of milk and unrefined Okinawan sugar.

**Difficulty Level ★**

**Prep time: 20 minutes**

## Ingredients

Milk *Kanten*
 2 Tbsp  granulated sugar
 60 ml  water
 1 envelope ($^1/_{10}$ oz/4 g) *kanten*, agar
 1  cup soymilk

Black *Kanten*
 1$^1/_2$ oz (40 g)  *kokuto**
 250 ml  water
 1  envelope ($^1/_8$ oz/4 g) *kanten*, agar

Decoration
 Black peas, boiled
 Kiwi
 Litchee

Sugar syrup
 3 Tbsp  granulated sugar
 80 ml  water

*unrefined black Okinawan sugar
(Substitute with molasses sugar)

**(serves 6)**

## Directions

① Make milk jelly. Put water, granulated sugar and agar powder in a saucepan, and bring to a boil. Cook and stir until the sugar and agar granules are dissolved.

② Transfer to a shallow square container and chill until set.

③ Make black sugar jelly. Put *kokuto*, water and agar in a saucepan and bring to a boil. Cook and stir until the sugar and agar granules are dissolved. Transfer to a shallow square container and chill until set. Make syrup. Put sugar and water in a saucepan, and heat until the sugar is completely dissolved. Let cool.

④ Cut jelly into cubes and arrange on a serving dish. Decorate with peas and fruits. Pour over sugar syrup.

# Cherry Compote with Soymilk Kanten

**Plain *kanten* jelly and sweet, stewed cherries compliment each other.**

**Difficulty Level ★★**

**Prep time: 20 minutes**

## Ingredients

Cherry Compote

    10 oz (250 g)  black cherries

    300 ml  red wine

    5 oz (140 g)  granulated sugar

    100 ml  water

    2  Tbsp kirsch

Milk *Kanten*

    $1^1/_2$ Tbsp  granulated sugar

    150 ml  water

    1  envelope (1/8 oz/4 g) *kanten**,

      agar granules

    400 ml  soymilk

    Kirsch

    Mint sprigs

**(serves 6)**

## Directions

① In a saucepan heat red wine to a boil. Add sugar, water, then cherries, and cook for 10 minutes over low heat.

Transfer cherries and liquid to a bowl over ice water, and let cool. Add kirsch, and chill for 6 hours or overnight.

② Make milk *kanten*. Put water, sugar and *kanten* granules in a saucepan and bring to a boil. Cook slowly for 4 - 5 minutes over low heat, stirring constantly. Add soymilk and return to boil.

③ Let cool slightly, and add kirsch. Pour into a mold and chill until set. Break *kanten* into pieces and arrange in a serving bowl. Top with cherry compote and pour over the liquid. Decorate with a mint sprig.

# Pear Souffle

**Flavorful pear puree blended with *tofu* turns into a set, cold souffle.
The trick is how to prepare the mold.**

## Ingredients

6 oz (180 g) canned pears
3 1/2 oz (100 g) soft *tofu*
1 oz (30 g) granulated sugar
Meringue
  2 egg whites
  1 1/2 oz (40 g) granulated sugar
150 ml heavy/whipping cream
Decoration
  Pear
  Pistachios

**(yields 3)**

### Do-Ahead Tips

◆Wrap *tofu* in a kitchen towel and microwave for 1-1.5 minutes; let stand to drain.
◆Secure card around souffle dish to stand about 1" (3 cm) above the rim.

## Directions

① Puree pear with drained *tofu* and sugar in a food processor. In a bowl, beat egg whites until thick but still runny. Add granulated sugar, and beat until stiff.

② Whip heavy/whipping cream until thick, and fold into pear puree.

③ Divide meringue into half portions, and fold into the pear mixture, one portion at a time.

④ Fill prepared souffle dish with the mixture, and smooth top. Chill at least 4 hours until set. Serve decorated with sliced pear and chopped pistachios.

# Cold Peach Soup

**A perfect summer dessert. Light and delicate soymilk "soup" adds to the flavor of peach.**

Difficulty Level ★

Prep time: 20 minutes

## Ingredients

300 ml  water
3$\frac{1}{2}$ oz (100 g)  granulated sugar
5  peach halves (canned)
70 ml  white wine
70 ml  soymilk
1 Tbsp  heavy/whipping cream
1 Tbsp  lemon juice
Yellow peaches
Plums
Raspberries
Blueberries
Crushed ice
**(serves 4-5)**

## Directions

① Make sugar syrup. Put the water and granulated sugar in a saucepan, and heat just until the sugar dissolves. Remove from heat and let cool.

② In an electric blender, put drained peaches, wine, soymilk, heavy/whipping cream, cooled sugar syrup and lemon juice. Puree until smooth.

③ In a serving bowl, put crushed ice and the "soup". Arrange the fruits cut into chunks on it . Add lime wedge to serve.

# Fruit and Milk Balls

**Enjoy the colorful effect and harmony of flavors.**

**Difficulty Level ★**

**Prep time: 20 minutes**

## Ingredients

1³/₄ oz (50 g)  rice flour for dumpling

1¹/₂ oz (40 g)  soft *tofu*

¹/₂ -1  Tbsp water

1  dozen red cherries, stoned

1  dozen black cherries, stoned

1  white peach, diced

¹/₄  honeydew melon, scooped

Blueberries

Sweet condensed milk

Kirsch

**(serves 4)**

## Do-Ahead Tips

◆Wrap *tofu* in a kitchen towel and microwave for 1-1.5 minutes; let stand to drain.

◆Prepare fruits and keep refrigerated until use.

## Directions

① In a bowl, combine rice flour, *tofu* and the water. Knead until the dough becomes as soft as an earlobe.

② Using your palms, form the dough into balls slightly smaller than cherries. Cook in boiling water. When they float to the surface, plunge them into ice water to cool.

③ In a bowl, place all the fruits and dumplings, and dress with condensed milk and kirsch. Serve in a fluted glass.

**An unexpectedly delicious way to serve assorted fruits.**

Difficulty Level ★

Prep time: 20 minutes

## Ingredients

1³/₄ oz (50 g)  rice flour for dumpling

1¹/₂ oz (40 g)  soft *tofu*

¹/₂ -1  Tbsp water

1  orange, peeled and diced

1  dozen raspberries

Caramel Sauce

  3 oz (80 g)  granulated sugar

  3 Tbsp  water

  3 Tbsp  hot water

**(serves 4)**

## Directions

① Make rice dumplings referring to the previous page, Steps 1 to 2.

② Make caramel sauce. Heat water with granulated sugar to a boil; simmer until golden. Remove heat and carefully stir in hot water. Protect your hand with a cotton glove or mitten from hot splashes.

③ In a serving dish, arrange fruits and dumplings. Pour over the caramel sauce.

*Edamame*, or young green soybeans, are a long-time favorite among the Japanese. Here, they are turned into a sweet and creamy sauce with a fresh green color.

**Difficulty Level ★★**

**Prep time: 20 minutes**

## Ingredients

Soymilk Mousse
  1 Tbsp (10 g)  gelatin
    powder
  300 ml  soymilk
  2  eggs, separated
  1³/₄ oz (50 g)  granulated
    sugar
*Edamame* Soup
  10¹/₂ oz (300 g)  *edamame**
  3¹/₂ oz (100 g)
    granulated sugar
  200 ml  water
  400 ml  soymilk
  100 ml  heavy/whipping
    cream
Topping
  Chinese wolfberries
  Pine nuts
  Star anise
* young soybeans in pods

**(serves 4)**

## Do-Ahead Tips

◆Remove pods of *edamame*, and boil 5-6 minutes until tender.

◆Soak the gelatin powder in 2 Tbsp water (extra) for 3-5 minutes.

## Directions

① In a food processor, puree cooked *edamame*, granulated sugar, water and soymilk.

② Strain into a saucepan, and cook over low heat stirring in heavy/whipping cream. Bring to a boil, and remove from heat. Transfer to a shallow metal container, and chill for 1 hour.

③ Make mousse. Heat soymilk just until it starts to bubble; set aside.

④ In a bowl, beat together egg yolks and half amount of sugar until pale. Stir in soymilk gradually. Stir

in softened gelatin. Place the bowl over ice water, and stir until slightly thickened.

⑤ In a separate bowl, whisk egg whites until foamy. Add remaining sugar, and whisk until stiff.

⑥ Fold half portion of the meringue into gelatin mixture. Fold in remaining meringue.

Transfer to a metal container and chill until set.

⑦ In a serving bowl, place scooped mousse and pour *edamame* sauce generously. Sprinkle with Chinese wolfberries, pine nuts and star anise.

# Taiwanese Tofu Pudding

Pronounced as Dou-hwa, this is a popular Chinese dessert whose name means "bean blossom". Here, with a pungent ginger flavor.

**Difficulty Level ★**

**Prep time: 20 minutes**

## Ingredients

1³/₄ oz (50 g)  granulated sugar
1  envelope (¹/₁₀ oz /3 g) *kanten* (agar)
350 ml  soymilk
Ginger Syrup
  3¹/₄ oz (90 g)  granulated sugar
  300 ml  water
  1 Tbsp  ginger juice
  7-8  slices gingerroot
1¹/₂ oz (40 g)  each, garbanzo, white, and red kidney beans (canned)
Mint leaves
White ear fungi, optional

## (serves 6)

## Do-Ahead Tips

◆Soften white ear fungi by soaking in hot water for 3-5 minutes.

## Directions

① Make pudding. Heat water, sugar and *kanten* slowly to a boil.
When *kanten* is completely dissolved, stir in soymilk. Pour into a mold and let stand to set. (*Kanten* sets at room temperature.)

② Make ginger syrup. In a saucepan, heat granulated sugar and water until the sugar is dissolved. Remove from heat just before boiling. While hot, add ginger juice and sliced ginger. Chill.

③ Add drained beans to the syrup, and mix well.
④ In a serving dish, place scoops of the set pudding and beans. Pour over ginger syrup, and add mint leaves and  white ear fungi.

# Chinese Almond Tofu

**A combination of sour sauce and creamy pudding, featuring the famous Chinese dessert.**

**Difficulty Level ★★**

**Prep time: 20 minutes**

## Ingredients (serves 4-6)

1 Tbsp (10 g)  gelatin powder
400ml  soymilk
3$^1$/$_2$ oz (100 g)  granulated sugar
3 - 4  drops almond extract
Kiwi Sauce
  2$^1$/$_4$ oz (60 g)  granulated sugar
  100 ml  water
  6  kiwi fruit
Kiwi slices, for decoration

## Do-Ahead Tips

◆Soak gelatin powder in 1$^1$/$_2$
Tbsp water (extra) for 3-5
minutes.

## Directions

① In a saucepan, heat soymilk
with granulated sugar. When
the sugar is dissolved, remove
from heat just before boiling.
Add almond extract.

② Stir softened gelatin into the
soymilk mixture. Strain into a
bowl, and stir until thickened
over ice water.
In a separate bowl, whip
heavy/whipping cream until
slightly thickened.

③ Add soymilk mixture to
whipped cream, and combine
well. Pour into serving glasses.
Make kiwi sauce. In a saucepan,
heat the sauce ingredients until
the sugar is dissolved. Remove
from heat and let cool.
④ Trim away seed section of
kiwis, and puree in a food
processor. Chill. Pour into the
glass and decorate with kiwi
slices.

# Coconut Tapioca Soup

**Delight in fun tasting refreshing muscat along with the special texture of tapioca pearls.**

**Difficulty Level ★**

**Prep time: 15 minutes**

## Ingredients

1¹⁄₂ oz (40 g)  tapioca pearls
400 ml  soymilk
4¹⁄₂ oz (130 g)  coconut milk
3¹⁄₂ oz (100 g)  granulated sugar
1 Tbsp  sweet osmanthus wine
¹⁄₂  pear
1¹⁄₂  dozen muscat
2 ³⁄₄ oz (80 g)  watermelon

**(serves 4)**

## Directions

① Soak tapioca in ample water (extra) for about 10 minutes; drain.
Cut pear and watermelon into chunks.

② In a saucepan, put water (extra) and drained tapioca. Cook for 20-30 minutes over low heat until the tapioca pearls are transparent. Drain and wash under running water to remove extra sliminess; drain.
In saucepan, heat soymilk, coconut milk and granulated sugar until the sugar is dissolved. Turn off heat just before boiling, and let cool.

③ Stir in sweet osmanthus wine, and chill for 1 hour.
Place fruits and tapioca in serving glass, and pour coconut mixture over them.

**Known as _kudzumochi_, this is a centuries-old Japanese tea accompaniment.
Here, sesame sauce is used in place of molasses.**

Difficulty Level ★

Prep time: 10 minutes

## Ingredients

3¹/₂ oz (100 g) _kudzu-ko_, arrowroot
  powder
5 oz (140 g) granulated sugar
260 ml soymilk
200 ml water
Black Sesame Sauce
  1³/₄ oz (50 g) black sesame paste
  1-2 Tbsp boiling water
  1 Tbsp honey
Fig
**(serves 4)**

## Directions

① In a bowl, put _kudzu-ko_ and sugar, and gradually add soymilk and
water. Combine with your fingers. Blend until all the lumps
disappear and the dough is smooth and thick.

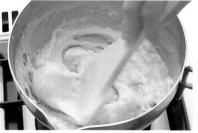 

③ Make black sesame sauce.
Add boiling water and honey to
sesame paste, and blend well.
Cut _kudzumochi_ into triangles,
and pour over black sesame
sauce. Serve with a wedged fig.

② Transfer to a saucepan, and cook over high heat scraping the
bottom constantly, until pasty. Immediately transfer to a shallow
metal container, and chill.

# Milky Warabi-Mochi

These soft-as-*tofu*, morsels are irresistible you when served with aromatic soy flour and molasses.

**Difficulty Level ★**

**Prep time: 10 minutes**

## Ingredients

3$^1/_2$ oz (100 g)  *warabi-ko*\*

200 ml  water

200 ml  soymilk

2 oz (60 g)  granulated sugar

Soy flour\*

*Kuromitsu* or molasses

\*Also sold under the name of *warabimochi-ko*.

\*May be sold under the name of *kinako*.

**(serves 6)**

## Directions

① In a bowl, put *warabi-ko* and gradually stir in little water. Blend well until all the lumpy powder disappears. Add remaining water, blend well, and add soymilk.

② When the mixture is thick and smooth, add sugar and whisk vigorously.

③ Strain into a saucepan. Cook and stir over medium heat. Use a wooden spatula to scrape off from the bottom of pan. Stir vigorously as it thickens. When it becomes elastic, remove from heat and let cool slightly.

④ While hot, transfer to a moistened metal container, and chill until set. Holding some of the mixture in one hand, squeeze off a bite-size portion, and cutting with a knife, drop into ice water. Drain and serve with soybean powder and molasses.

# DRINKS & SHAKES

**Here are easy-to-make soymilk drinks, to be arranged with your favorite ingredients.**

**Cappuccino**

Difficulty Level ★

Prep time: 10 minutes

**Mochappuccino**

Difficulty Level ★

Prep time: 10 minutes

## Mochappuccino

**The popular combination of strong coffee and frothy milk.**

### Ingredients
360 ml  soymilk
1 1/2 Tbsp  instant coffee
2 Tbsp  hot water
Steamed Milk
  80 ml  soymilk
Topping
  Instant coffee
**(serves 2)**

### Directions
① In a saucepan, dissolve instant coffee in hot water. Add soymilk and heat until it starts bubbling. Do not boil.

② Make steamed milk. Microwave soymilk in a medium glass bowl, covered, for about 40 seconds until lukewarm. Using an electric beater, whisk for 2 minutes until fluffy.
③ Pour soymilk coffee into serving cups. Spoon in steamed milk, and sprinkle with instant coffee.

## Cappuccino

**Add a touch of cinnamon.**

### Ingredients
360 ml soymilk
1 1/2 Tbsp  instant coffee
2 Tbsp  hot water
1  cinnamon stick
Steamed Milk
  80 ml  soymilk
Topping
  Ground cinnamon
**(serves 2)**

### Directions
① In a saucepan, dissolve instant coffee in hot water. Add cinnamon stick and soymilk.  Heat until it starts bubbling. Do not boil.
② Make steamed milk. Microwave soymilk in a medium glass bowl, covered, for about 40 seconds until luke-warm. Using an electric beater, whisk for 2 minutes until frothy.
③ Pour soymilk coffee into serving cups. Spoon in steamed milk, and sprinkle with ground cinnamon.

**Almond Cafe au Lait**

Difficulty Level ★

Prep time: 10 minutes

Green Tea Cappuccino

Difficulty Level ★

Prep time: 10 minutes

# Green Tea Cappuccino

**The bitterness of green tea is mellowed by the mild and frothy soymilk.**

## Ingredients

360 ml  soymilk

1 Tbsp  powdered green tea

  1 tsp  granulated sugar

  2 Tbsp  hot water

Steamed Milk

  80 ml  soymilk

Topping

  Powdered green tea

**(serves 2)**

## Directions

① Combine powdered green tea and granulated sugar. Add hot water and stir until dissolved and smooth.

② In a saucepan, heat soymilk and green tea mixture, stirring constantly. Turn off heat just below the boiling point. Make steamed milk. Microwave soymilk in a medium glass bowl, covered, for about 40 seconds until lukewarm. Using an electric beater, whisk for 2 minutes until frothy.

③ Pour soymilk coffee into serving cups. Spoon in steamed milk, and sprinkle with powdered green tea.

# Almond Cafe au Lait

**The aroma of roasted almonds and the mildness of milk enhance each other.**

## Ingredients

$1\frac{1}{2}$ (40 g) oz  sliced almonds

200 ml  soymilk

300 ml  strong coffee

Almond extract or amaretto

Steamed Milk

  80 ml  soymilk

Sliced almonds, roasted

**(serves 2)**

## Directions

① In a saucepan, heat sliced almonds and soymilk for 2-3 minutes over low heat. Cover and let steam for about 5 minutes.

② Strain and return to the saucepan. Add coffee and heat just until the mixture reaches the boiling point.

③ Make steamed milk. Microwave soymilk in a medium glass bowl, covered, for about 40 seconds until lukewarm. Using an electric beater, whisk for 2 minutes until frothy.

④ Pour into serving cups and top with roasted almond slices.

**Cafe Macchiato**

Difficulty Level ★
Prep time: 10 minutes

**Iced Milk Tea**

Difficulty Level ★
Prep time: 10 minutes

# Cafe Macchiato

**Strong coffee with bittersweet caramel syrup.**

## Ingredients

Caramel Syrup
  3 Tbsp  heavy/whipping cream
  1¹/₂ Tbsp  granulated sugar
  1¹/₂ Tbsp  water
360 ml  strong coffee
Steamed Milk
  100 ml  soymilk

**(serves 2)**

## Directions

① Make caramel syrup. Put heavy/whipping cream in an ovenproof dish, and microwave uncovered for 25 seconds.

② In a separate dish, blend sugar and water. Microwave uncovered for 3-4 minutes until lightly browned.

③ Gradually add cream to the syrup, protecting your hands with cotton gloves since it is burning hot. (This caramel syrup keeps 2-10 weeks if refrigerated. Warm in a double boiler when using.)

④ Make steamed milk as for cappuccino (page 78, Step 2).

⑤ Brew strong coffee, and spoon on the steamed milk. Drizzle caramel syrup over it.

# Iced Milk Tea

**Soymilk goes with black tea very well.**

## Ingredients

2  Earl Grey teabags
250 ml  boiling water
60 ml soymilk
Crushed ice
Mint sprigs

**(serves 2)**

## Directions

① Place teabags in a warmed teapot. Pour in boiling water and let brew for 5 minutes to make strong tea.

② Fill serving goblets with crushed ice in a heap. Pour hot tea over it, then pour in soymilk gently. Garnish with a mint sprig. Stir when drinking.

**Green Tea Shake**

Difficulty Level ★

Prep time: 10 minutes

**Orange Lassi**

Difficulty Level ★

Prep time: 10 minutes

# Orange Lassi

**The famous Indian milkshake, here with honey.**

## Ingredients

200 ml  soymilk

100 ml  plain yogurt

1¹/₂-2 Tbsp  honey

50 ml  orange juice

Crushed ice

Orange segments, optional

Mint sprigs, optional

**(serves 2)**

## Directions

① In an electric blender, blend soymilk, yogurt, honey and orange juice.

② Fill serving goblet with crushed ice. Pour lassi over it. Garnish with an orange segment and mint sprig, if preferred.

# Green Tea Shake

**Use commercial green tea ice cream for quick preparation.**

## Ingredients

3 oz (75 g) green tea ice cream

300 ml soymilk

Decoration

  Green tea ice cream

**(serves 2)**

## Directions

① In an electric blender, mix all the ingredients, omitting ice cream for topping, until well blended.

② Pour into serving glasses. Spoon in ice cream.

**Berry Smoothie**

**Peach Smoothie**

# SMOOTHIES

**This "drinkable dessert" with a crunchy texture
can be made quickly using frozen fruits.**

**Citrus Smoothie**

# Peach Smoothie

### Ingredients

1  white peach
250 ml  soymilk
1 Tbsp  honey
1 Tbsp  plain yogurt
Topping
  Cornflakes
  Peach slices

**(serves 2)**

### Directions

① Peel and cut peach into
chunks. Place in a freezer bag
and let freeze in a freezer.
② In an electric blender, mix
frozen peach and all remaining
ingredients omitting topping.
③ Pour into serving glasses and
top with cornflakes and peach
slices.

# Berry Smo

### Ingredients

8  raspberries
3  strawberries
1  dozen blueberries
250 ml  soymilk
1$^1/_2$ Tbsp  honey
1 Tbsp  plain yogurt
Topping
  Raspberries
  Blueberries

**(serves 2)**

Difficulty Level ★

Prep time: 5 minutes

**Tropical Smoothie**

# Tropical Smoothie

## Ingredients

$^1/_2$ banana
3 oz (80 g) pineapple
$^1/_4$ mango
1 Tbsp plain yogurt
250 ml soymilk
Topping
 Starfruit, sliced

**(serves 2)**

## Directions

① Remove skin and unnecessary parts of the fruits. Cut them into chunks and put in a freezer bag. Let freeze in a freezer.

② In an electric blender, mix the frozen fruits and all remaining ingredients omitting the topping.

③ Pour into serving glasses and top with starfruit slices.

# Citrus Smoothie

## Directions

① Put berries in a freezer bag, and let freeze in a freezer.

② In an electric blender, mix frozen berries and all remaining ingredients omitting the topping.

③ Pour into serving glasses and top with raspberries and blueberries.

## Ingredients

1 orange
1 grapefruit
250 ml soymilk
2 Tbsp honey
1 Tbsp plain yogurt
Topping
 Orange slices
 Lime rind

**(serves 2)**

## Directions

① Skin off orange and grapefruit, and put in a freezer bag. Let freeze in a freezer.

② In an electric blender, mix frozen citrons and all remaining ingredients omitting the topping.

③ Pour into serving glasses and top with orange slices and lime rind.

Difficulty Level ★

Prep time: 5 minutes

**Tofu and Prune Shake**

**Green Veggie Shake**

Difficulty Level ★

Prep time: 5 minutes

**Banana and Avocado Shake**

Difficulty Level ★

Prep time: 5 minutes

# HEALTHY SHAKES

**Delicious yet nutritious drinks containing vitamins and minerals, and vegetable protein.**

# Banana and Avocado Shake

### Ingredients

$^{1}/_{2}$ banana
1 small apple
$^{1}/_{4}$ avocado
2 tsp lemon juice
1 Tbsp honey
250 ml soymilk
$^{1}/_{2}$ cup ice cubes
Decoration
  Lime wedges

**(serves 2)**

### Directions

① In an electric blender, mix all the ingredients omitting the topping.
② Pour into serving glasses, and garnish with lime wedges.

# Tofu and Prune Shake

### Ingredients

$1^{3}/_{4}$ oz (50 g) soft *tofu*
1 prune, pitted
200 ml soymilk
1 small apple
1 Tbsp honey
Decoration
  Apple slices

**(serves 2)**

### Directions

① Core the apple.
② In an electric blender, mix all the ingredients omitting the apple slices.
③ Pour into serving glasses, and garnish with apple slices.

# Green Veggie Shake

### Ingredients

$^{1}/_{4}$ celery stalk
$^{3}/_{4}$ oz (20 g) spinach
1 small apple
250 ml soymilk
1 Tbsp honey
Decoration
  Celery leaves

**(serves 2)**

### Directions

① String the celery, and cut into chunks. Chop the spinach. Core the apple.
② In an electric blender, mix all the ingredients omitting the decoration.
③ Pour into serving glasses and garnish with celery leaves.

# Nutrition & Health Benefits of Soybean

For many years, soybeans and soybean products have been a staple source of protein for the Japanese. It is obvious from the fact that soy beans used be called, "the meat from the soil" just until recently, since the Japanese once had meat taboo.

Soybean protein provides all the essential amino acids that are needed for our health. Besides the complete vegetable protein, soy beans are especially rich in calcium, iron, magnesium and polyunsaturated fatty acids, including linoleic and linolenic fatty acids which are essential for good circulation of the human body.

Traditional Japanese soybean products include soymilk, *tofu*, *miso* (soybean paste), soy sauce, *kinako* (soy flour), and *natto* (fermented soybeans). Besides, there is a by-product called *okara*, which is valued highly for its nutrients and dietary fiber. In the process of making *tofu*, soybeans are soaked in water overnight, crushed and cooked, then strained to divide into soymilk and *okara*. Soymilk is usually made into *tofu*, by adding a calcium surfcate to curdle, and then pressed into cakes.

*Tofu* and soymilk have been and still are one of the most popular food in Japan because they are easier to digest compared to whole soybeans, therefore used widely in diets for babies, those with digestive problems, and seniors in most Asian countries. This book is aimed to show how to take in these nutrients as a delicious dessert, not only as a substitute for cow's milk. Use non-dairy cream or vegetable oil, if needed, and adjust yourself!

## The Three Spotlighted Nutrients Found in Soybean Products

### Calcium

Calcium is one of the vital minerals for building up bones and teeth. It is known that deficiency in calcium may result in such mental conditions as irritability or nervousness.

Soymilk and *tofu* contain calcium naturally, and *tofu* has added calcium too (3-ounce/ 100-gram firm *tofu* contains 120 mg calcium ). The good quality soy protein accelerates its absorption.

### Isoflavone

Regarded neither as a vitamin or mineral, this phytochemical has been often talked about these days. Recent studies show that isoflavone seems to work the same way as estrogen, a female hormone, and lessens hot flashes or other menopausal symptoms. Also, isoflavone helps calcium stay inside the bones, thus preventing osteoporosis.

Isoflavone can be found in other foods, but much less than in soy products. Note that *kinako*, or soy flour, is exceedingly rich in isoflavone whereas soy sauce and soy oil have none.

### Oligosaccharide

The glucide that gives the subtle sweetness to soymilk or *tofu* consists of oligosaccharide. Oligosaccharide is said to prevent bad bacteria growth inside the intestines, which may trigger diseases or fast aging. Researches show that it activates intestines, improves immune system, or break down carcinogen.

Oligosaccharide serves as a "food" for bifidobacteria, an active agent that fights against bad bacteria in the intestines, thus maintains intestinal health.

## VARIETIES OF SOYMILK

Generally, there are two types in soymilk, natural and prepared. For drinking, you may find prepared type acceptable, but for cooking uses as a substitute for cow's milk, either of them will do. Compare the tastes and choose your favorite.

## VARIETIES OF TOFU

*Tofu* comes in two types, firm and soft. In the final process of making *tofu*, soymilk is strained through a cloth, either cotton or silk. If strained through cotton, the finished texture is firm, while silk makes soft and smooth cake.

## MORE SOYFOODS

*Okara*, a by-product of *tofu* making, is gaining attention for its protein and fiber content. *Okara* adds crunchiness to cookies and donuts besides upgrading nutritional value.

Although not as popular as *tofu* or soymilk, *kinako*, or soy flour, is a great way to take in complete protein and other minerals. According to the USDA Human Nutrition Information Service Agriculture Handbook No. 8-16, *okara* has the following nutrient composition per 3$^1/_2$ oz (100 grams):

### Nutrient Composition of *Okara*

| | |
|---|---|
| Kcal | 77 |
| protein | 3.2 g |
| Carbohydrate | 12.5 g |
| Fiber | 4.1 |
| Calcium | 80 |
| Iron | 1.3 |
| Thiamin | 0.02 mg |
| Riboflavin | 0.02 mg |
| Niacin | 0.1 mg |

# KITCHEN UTENSILS FOR MAKING SWEETS

## Oblong Baking Pans/Container

Baking tins can also be used widely in preparation of sweets, such as cooling hot cooked ingredients, because metals conduct heat quickly. Have a large choice of depths and sizes.

## Bowls

Bowls come in metal or ovenproof glassware. Stainless steel bowls convey heat quickly, and ideal for chilling or warming the bottoms. Meanwhile, glassware can be used for microwave cooking or baking. Choose the correct bowl for each preparation to make cooking easier.

## Spatulas

For efficient mixing, a wooden spatula plays an important role when cooking over heat whereas a rubber spatula is used to fold in fluffy ingredients and scrape the bowl. Choose a heatproof rubber spatula for multiple use.

## Dough Cutter

This versatile cooking tool can either cut the butter in flour without conveying the warmth of your hands, or for transferring content of a bowl in a single motion.

## Beaters

An essential tool when preparing sweets when creaming or whipping is required. To select a balloon whisk, take one with a thick handle and many wires. An electric beater is handy with a speed control.

## Rolling Pin

Wooden rolling pins are most popular, but marble ones stay cool and are easier to work with. Besides using to roll out pie or cookie dough, you can crush crackers or cookies into fine grains with a rolling pin.

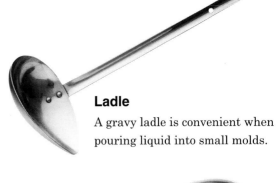

## Ladle

A gravy ladle is convenient when pouring liquid into small molds.

## Strainer

This is for draining liquid or sieving light liquid.

## Fine Strainer

Large cone-shaped sieve with fine holes called Chinois has a large area to work with a spoon. Good for making a smooth texture for ice cream.

## Tea Strainer

This is mainly used to sprinkle powdered sugar or cocoa evenly over finished sweets.

## Measuring Equipment

In preparation of sweets, accurate measuring equipment makes a difference. A level tablespoon (Tbsp) measures 15 ml, and a level teaspoon (tsp) measures 5 ml. American cup measures 254ml, which is adopted in this book.

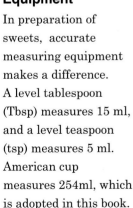

## Brush

Flat and wide brushes are used to apply glaze or syrup over pies and sponges.

## Electric Scale

For making sweets, measuring is very important. An electric scale measures by one gram, up to one or two kilograms (2-4 lbs). For precise measuring, weigh dry ingredients before sifting, and butter before softening.

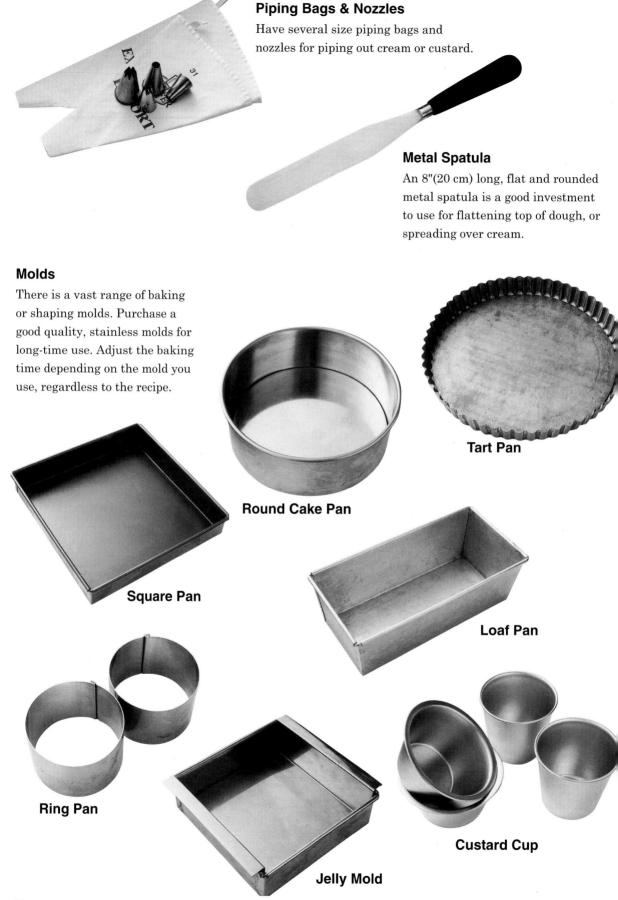

### Piping Bags & Nozzles

Have several size piping bags and nozzles for piping out cream or custard.

### Metal Spatula

An 8"(20 cm) long, flat and rounded metal spatula is a good investment to use for flattening top of dough, or spreading over cream.

### Molds

There is a vast range of baking or shaping molds. Purchase a good quality, stainless molds for long-time use. Adjust the baking time depending on the mold you use, regardless to the recipe.

**Tart Pan**

**Round Cake Pan**

**Square Pan**

**Loaf Pan**

**Ring Pan**

**Custard Cup**

**Jelly Mold**

# Glossary

## Batter

Uncooked, runny mixture for cakes, pancakes, or coating for deep-frying.

## Beat

To make mixture smooth and evenly blended, using a vigorous motion to incorporate air. A spoon, wire whisk, hand beater or electric mixer is used.

## Blend

To mix ingredients until they are thoroughly combined.

## Brulee

To burn a sugar coating beneath a broiler or using a burner until it is caramelized to form a crisp glaze.

## Chop

To cut food into small pieces, but usually not as finely as mincing, using a knife or a food processor.

## Clafoutis

Original French word for fruit gratin.

## Cream

To beat ingredients until light and fluffy. Usually used for blending butter with sugar.

## Double boiler

A deep, cone-shaped pot to moderately warm a bowl or pot. Substitute with a wide saucepan filled with hot water, over low heat.

## Dough

A flour mixture, soft but firm enough to hold its shape.

## Dust

To coat food lightly with a dry, powdery ingredient such as sugar or cocoa powder.

## Fold

To combine ingredients gently, retaining their volumes by adding the lighter ingredient to the heavier one, and mixing with a figure eight motion.

## Fry

To cook food in hot fat or oil. Pancakes should be fried in oil just enough to cover the bottom of pan, while donuts, churros and beignets should be deep-fried, or cooked in enough oil to cover.

## Gelatin

A setting substance to make jelly, made from boiled animal bones. Available in leaf or powdered form, with the former being used to make a clearer jelly, needs about 10% less than the latter. If using leaf type gelatin, soak in ample water to cover for at least 10 minutes until softened, and then drain well before stirring into warmed food.

## Green tea

Powdered green tea or *matcha*, praised for its aroma and fresh color.
Available in small cans. Store refrigerated.

## Grease

To coat the inside of a mold or baking pan with oil or butter so that food can be taken out easily after being cooked.

## *Kanten*

Agar, a seaweed-based, zero-calorie vegetarian alternative to gelatin. *Kanten* is softened in water and boiled for a few minutes before being added to juice or flavor. Unlike gelatin, *kanten* jelly does not liquify under high temperatures. Available in powder form at Asian or health food stores.

## *Kinako*

Soy flour made by finely grinding roasted soybeans. Unlike many flours, it is high in digestible protein and low in carbohydrates, and therefore gathering attention from dieticians. Available at health food stores.

# Glossary

## Meringue

Light and airy mixture of white part of eggs and sugar, made by vigorous whisking, to be baked on its own or as a raising ingredient for cakes and mousses. For a successful meringue, use a clean bowl and whisk that have no trace of oil or water, and do not add sugar before the first whisking when you need a stiff meringue.

## Mousse

A light and fluffy, chilled dessert or appetizer made of whisked eggs, milk or cream, and/or sugar.

## *Okara*

In making *tofu*, soybeans are soaked in water overnight, crushed and cooked, then strained to divide into soymilk and *okara*.

Although a little too fibrous and dry to eat on its own, it is known as a health food rich in essential nutrients, and therefore makes a good addition to baked foods. See page 87 for more information.

## Parchment

A non-stick baking paper to be used to line baking pans.

## Puree

To crush solid food until it is almost liquefied with lessened volume. In confectionary cooking, purees are sometimes sieved to make a smoother texture.

## Sesame seeds

These aromatic seeds were once regarded as a medicine in Egypt two thousand years ago. Nowadays they are widely used in both savory and sweet dishes. Sesame seeds are sold in various forms including raw, toasted, ground, and paste, each available in yellowish white and black. Keep toasted or ground seeds in a freezer if you use them only once in a while.

## Sieve

To pass ingredients through a sieve or strainer in order to get a smooth texture without lumps.

## Skimmed milk

A non-fat milk powder retaining other nutrients, often used in a low-fat diet.

## Souffle

A light, savory or sweet dish based on beaten egg whites to incorporate much air. Although souffle is originally a cooked dish that can be deflated in a few minutes, a souffle "effect" can be created by adding a removable extention to molds as shown on page 68.

## Syrup

A thick sweet liquid made basically with sugar and water, to be mixed with other foods or served on top of desserts.

## *Tofu*

Also known as soybean curd, *tofu* is made from boiled soybeans. Soymilk is set with calcium salt, a curdling agent, therefore *tofu* is a good source of calcium. After opening the package, be sure to fill it with water.

## *Tonyu*

Japanese word for soymilk, as "to (pronounced as in *toe*)" means beans, "*nyu*", milk. *Tonyu* can be made into *tofu* by blending with *nigari*, a natural thickening agent derived from sea salt, and heated carefully just as if you were making egg custard.

## Whisk

To blend ingredients vigorously, especially cream and egg, using a metal whisk that incorporates air into the mixture.

## *Yuzu*

A sour and fragrant citrus fruit from Japan. Its uneven, yellow rind is shredded or grated to use as a flavoring as well as its juice. Good for cakes, sorbets and drinks.